Praise for *John Kelly Samaritan:*

June W. Lamb, Author of *The Learning Journey*: This book is a splendid achievement in chronicling one man's journey through the fogbanks of life which drove him toward a greater degree of consciousness. I doubt that anyone could read it without becoming more aware of the world's need for bringing science, morality and spirituality together through <u>action</u>. John Kelly's example of courage in following his heart, mind and spirit, which forced him to leave the comfort of imposed moral and spiritual rule, is very moving. His story and success in making the world a better place challenges the reader to "do more."

Vincent Huening: John Kelly is common thread that ties together the social activism and justice movements locally and nationally. John's biography furthers the cause of restorative justice, and tells about leadership (challenging the status quo, developing willing followers), about reforming Christianity, about modern-day non-profit activism, about sainthood, and about education reform. I recommend this book as required reading for all university religious studies programs.

State Senator Jerry Hill: John Kelly has committed his life to helping those less fortunate. He has been a role model for the community, an exemplary citizen, and he has sensitized so many of us to the plight of our fellows. Our community is better because of John Kelly.

Vic Perrella: John Kelly is a St. Francis of Assisi of the twenty-first century.

Elaine Leeder, Author of *My Life with Lifers*: I think that as a single man in the world John created a far bigger family than any of us have in our blood families. I'm thrilled that John is being honored by his story being told. A biography is a way of cloning him; some way of noting what he has done. And some, hopefully, will pick up his example.

Sue Lempert: Samaritan House was a unique non-profit: the administrative costs were very low, they had many volunteers and they really were out to serve people not served in any other place. So to me, John Kelly was a big hero.

About the Author:

Tom Huening has been a Navy and TWA pilot, lawyer, CPA, commercial real estate investor and local politician. Tom hosted *Spiritual Choices*, a local TV program interviewing local and national spiritual leaders with disparate points of view. He shares a restorative justice interest with John Kelly.

Tom has four successful daughters and sons in law as well as nine grandchildren, and lives in San Mateo, California.

Also by Tom Huening:

Spiritual Choices: Putting the HERE in Hereafter

John Kelly
Samaritan

by

Tom Huening

06.19.14

Mitch,

Thanks. Tom

Spiritual Choices Publishing

Published by
Spiritual Choices Publishing, San Mateo, California, 2013
www.SpiritualChoices.com

Printed in the United States of America

Library of Congress Control Number: 2013901622

ISBN: 978-0-9817341-3-2 (pbk.)
ISBN: 978-0-9817341-4-9 (ebk.)

Acknowledgments:

John Kelly has scores of friends, all of whom have been willing to help. Many have agreed to be interviewed for attribution and are named in the book.

My initial editor Susan Shankle and editors A.V. Walters and her partner Rick have provided sound advice and careful scrutiny and encouraged me greatly.

My associate editor, brother Vince Huening and special friend and editor, Carol Perusse have been invaluable in their suggestions and support.

Quotes are substantially accurate but sometimes edited for clarity.

Errors, of course, are mine, all mine -- mea culpa.

For the many friends of John Kelly
who contributed to his biography

Contents

Preface v

Introduction 1

One — Growing Up in San Francisco 3

Two — Call To Be a Catholic Priest 9

Three — Serra High School in San Mateo, California 19

Four — John Turns in His Collar 33

Five — Samaritan House, Feeding the Hungry 41

Six — Albert Odom, an Early Success 49

Seven — Clothing the Naked, Housing the Homeless; Healing the Sick 59

Eight — Education and Service to Youth 71

Nine — Restorative Justice 87

Ten — Sam Vaughn Success Story 103

Eleven — Reforming Criminal Justice 111

Twelve — James Alexander Success Story 121

Thirteen — Thoughts on Religions 131

Conclusion 141

After Words — Personal Comments about John 145

Appendix A — Letters from San Quentin 153

Appendix B — Photos 165

The Faithful *pray* for the homeless, hungry, sick and imprisoned.
The Good *provide* shelter, food, healthcare and solace.

Preface

John Kelly removed and dropped his cassock to his feet. He had just finished saying Catholic Mass. As the weight of years of doubt and struggle lifted from his shoulders he began singing "Born Free" in his booming voice. John, however, was not alone in the privacy of his rectory room. He performed this dramatic renunciation of a twenty-five year priesthood career in front of the amazed and supportive congregation of St. Mark's parish in Belmont, California in 1979.

John had wrestled with his conscience, hoping he could fulfill his vocation and continue his life-long career as a priest. But after a long and painful struggle, witnessing the shortcomings of modern religion, he discovered he could not budge the Catholic bureaucracy to accept his form of social action. So he left his Mother Church behind in this disobedient, shocking, yet personally satisfying final act to work for social justice.

John is a 'fallen-away' former Roman Catholic priest. He didn't quit to get married. He wasn't de-frocked because of a scandal. His commitment to social justice exceeded and transcended that of his church. He felt his Mother Church had been co-opted by the organizational, bureaucratic model common to many organizations as they grow larger. He would not describe it this way but, in a way, he became holier than his Church. He followed the Jesus example that lived only a limited life in the early organizational church. John didn't fall away. He leapt away with a clear purpose and a passion for compassion.

There were no lightning bolts of instant enlightenment. John struggled with each life choice as do we all. John says he "didn't set out to be or do good." He says he was corralled into his various life situations. More likely he recognized and made it his job to fill those human needs.

Introduction

John Kelly is a Good Samaritan and much more. He is a spiritual superstar. You will not mistake John for evangelist Rick Warren or the late Billy Graham. Rather, you might not even notice him, and pass him by. Or more likely you might scurry out of his way as he clunks his walker down the sidewalk. He is tall, a youngish eighty-four, lanky with close cropped, unruly white hair and a usually scruffy short beard. He's neat, functionally dressed and has been described as good looking. He is serious. He's happy but smiles sparingly. He fakes crankiness. He is very intelligent and alert.

You may already know and love him because he has saved your life. Too bad if you haven't met him; you may not encounter another like him if you live a hundred years. To his eternal embarrassment he is sometimes compared to Jesus.

John is a champion of individuals in need wherever they may be. Certainly he has led many in his home town to care for the poor and hungry and disenfranchised. But his is an example to all cities and towns. John developed a major, mostly privately-funded, two-thousand-volunteer, non-profit organization. He is a leader working with community leaders to accomplish important social and spiritual goals. John has been part of our country's history of integration and the civil rights movement. He is a beacon of acceptance of all of God's creatures.

He has shown the way to forgive and redeem the imprisoned – even those incarcerated for serious crimes. He supports and helps those who are otherwise abandoned by today's society. He is mentor and father figure to some serious criminals whom he has helped return to peaceful, productive lives. Their stories are included here as part of John's story. He points out the fallacy of using only punishment to redress crime and the shortsightedness of not rehabilitating prisoners; mostly they return as our neighbors. John shows that restorative justice can work and his proof is in his friends who have changed and now contribute to society.

John demonstrates how an individual education plan works for youth on whom many have given up. He shows how responsible adult attention in sports, school and family can turn around gang bangers and set them on a success path.

John sets an example for all who are learning to practice compassion and forgiveness. Certainly I've learned and hope I have shared John's life lessons in this, the story of his life and works. For John, it is not about recognition but about following the example of Jesus and the great spiritual leaders of all time.

John is a humble guy. As host of a local TV interview program called *Spiritual Choices*, when I described John as the man I know who is most like Jesus, he was dismissive and embarrassed. When I asked if I could write his biography he looked uncomfortable. He said he was worried about his ego if a book were written about him. I assured him that I would say enough bad things about him to save him from getting a swelled head. On the (facetious) threat of the dangers of my writing an *un*authorized biography he reluctantly agreed to be interviewed for this book.

John has a fabulous memory and recalls details from very early in his life. Mostly John is about important issues – *people* issues – especially those related to social justice. He has little patience for bureaucratic shenanigans but you'd hardly know it as he sits through endless committee meetings with hardly a protest. He'll do whatever needs to be done to advance the cause of helping others. He is an inspiration to me and to many others, and, after reading the stories that follow, I expect he will inspire you as well.

John grew up faithful. His family believed in the Catholic Church. He was ordained a priest and faithfully served in a parish and in a high school.

John struggled with Church bureaucracy and hypocrisy and ultimately decided he could do more good by being less faithful. He prayed less and provided more.

One

Growing Up in San Francisco

As a child, John only remembers crying when his brother Donald was born. John was sent away, exiled, at the early age of three when Donald joined the family. He felt rejected and sad at a time when he was told to be happy and proud. For nearly two months John lived away from the family to ease the burden on his mother Elly. But as a youngster he felt abandoned and lonely. "I did not know how long I was to be gone or if I was ever coming back."

To this day, John wonders why his mom decided she could not handle John and his baby brother at the same time. She may have just felt overwhelmed. So John was dropped off to stay with his godmother in Oakland. **Nora Kyne** didn't have any kids and so was quite pleased to have John around. "All I know is that when I finally got back home I felt panic and wondered if I still belonged to my family." And, of course, John's mom was busy with the baby and his dad "didn't seem to know what was going on. On top of that, just after I got home I had to go to the hospital overnight to get my tonsils out, and this added to my feeling of abandonment."

What John remembers is that when he returned home he was a totally different kid. "I had nightmares and spooky dreams. The worst thing was, I kept throwing anger tantrums all over the place. I'd go off and scream – I was an angry little kid." John says his mother was a fine lady but she wanted law and order. She did not know what to do with John or how to control him. "And unfortunately her method became trying to intimidate me rather than trying to understand what was going on.

"She used to say, 'you're not a boy, you're really a girl' because boys didn't do what I was doing. And that really got to me – it stuck." Two vivid incidents: One day she chased John down the alley and John became trapped because he couldn't reach a high gate latch. She pinned him in the corner and dumped a bucket of cold water over him. She figured that was the way she'd make him stop acting out. "Then she took me downstairs and left me standing there in the basement, soaking wet, and for a long time she paid no attention to me.

"Finally, at age four or five, I did decide I had to change, after all that reminding that I was a girl instead of a boy." It was after another incident. One day John's mother actually put him in one of her dresses and made him walk out in the back yard all by himself. "Like an idiot I was ranting and hollering while walking around the yard in my mother's dress, calling more attention to myself.

"I became round-shouldered; I was tense as all get out. The combination of all this turmoil made me wonder, who am I? My self-image was really poor. It has affected me my whole life. Emotionally, it affected who I was."

While growing up, John's older brother Ray was always strong and aggressive. "He totally dominated my life. I was this pudgy little kid. I had no sense of being anybody."

When John graduated from the eighth grade he was five-foot-two, weighed 102 pounds and had a high squeaky voice. *(Now he is six-foot-three, weighs 200-something pounds and has a very deep voice.)* It all had a profound effect on him. Not until coming home after his third year in the seminary did he realize that finally he was taller than his brother. "I got cocky and it had a lot of significance to me."

These were difficult times for the family. John's dad, **Raymond Charles Kelly**, was just a nice guy. He was born in Menlo Park and grew up there with two sisters and two brothers. "He was just a mild, gentle human being." He worked as a traveling salesman and was gone about half the time. John's grandmother (dad's mom) was chronically unhappy, a very unhappy lady. And John's grandfather was this meek, mild guy "who just sat there and took it." And to a large degree that was what happened between John's folks. His mother was extremely aggressive, dominant, controlling. John said she was very frustrated because she wanted to be a career woman and that she had all kinds of talent but never got past the eighth grade. One of her dictums was: "You boys are going to make up for what I couldn't do." But since she had so much trouble controlling my older brother, "I became her hope." John was the smartest kid in the class and because of her expectation, "I never had my own identity."

Mother's Day has always been a challenge for John because he wants to feel good but doesn't have sense of warmth about his mom. He sensed that he needed to be good so he could make her look good. There was never a lot of unconditional love. "Mother's Day this year, my brother Donald called me and I just asked him, what was mom like for you? He had no problem with her and I sense that my other brothers had no problem either. But she was a problem for me."

John's family "went through hell" during the Great Depression. "I hate to tell you what our life style was like. We weren't always sure what we were going to do for dinner." Even though John's dad lost his salesman job and was around more, John's mother was still running the show. "Times were tough, but there were some amazing things about my folks – they knocked their tails off for us. Both of them had their teeth rot in their mouth because they could not afford to go to a dentist. They made unbelievable sacrifices for us to survive." One of John's favorite stories is about his mother's job as a part-time bookkeeper for a canned goods company in downtown San Francisco. Every once in a while they let her bring cans home. The cans had no labels so the family had no idea what was in them. When they got desperate those cans would be their dinner. "We'd be down in the basement shaking the cans. Some of the cans had fruit cocktail, some had spaghetti and some had dog food. But we never ate the dog food."

And so Elly Kelly, frustrated by an unfulfilled ambition and the poverty of the Depression, treaded water and did her best to raise John and his brothers.

In the mid-1930s the Kellys rented a beautiful house in San Francisco, a three story Victorian. The owner came to John's folks one day and said he had to sell so the family either had to buy or move. John's dad wasn't working at the time so panic set in. The asking price was $3,750. The Kellys talked the guy down to $3,250. They borrowed $500 from one of John's mother's friends who had some PG&E stock, made the down payment with it and ended up buying the house. (John's younger brother, a realtor, said it was recently on the market for $1,200,000.) John remembers that the roof leaked and almost every Saturday his dad was up on the roof repairing all the holes with tar, and they had buckets catching water. It was a mess – but they survived.

John's maternal grandmother, **Amania Jensen Poulsen,** was "one of the most beautiful human beings I've ever known. She was warm and effusive." His Danish grandparents were very aristocratic and his grandfather owned one of the largest brick factories in Denmark. Apparently his business partner "screwed him out of everything" and that's why they came to the United States. John's grandfather was an artist – he did the two paintings hanging on John's wall. One of the family legends is that "he had an exhibition at a Paris fair. They were well-to-do."

John thinks his mother suffered somewhat as a child of the formerly wealthy, and she probably spent a lot of time without parenting as her parents made the European social scene. She was used to the good life; then her family came here and they "were bouncing around trying to survive." John's grandfather became a house painter.

John said that World War II saved their family. John's dad became an asbestos worker and he joined a union. He made enough money for them finally to survive. Asbestos workers often got lung cancer. However, John's father, "wherever he got the idea, would put a mask on whenever he would work in tight quarters. When he got home the first thing he would do is flush his nostrils out." A lot of John's dad's co-workers died early in life but his dad lived to be eighty-six. John got a job as an asbestos helper during a couple of summers when he was on vacation from the seminary. One of his jobs after the war was converting one of the cruise liners back into being a cruise ship after temporary duty as a troop carrier. It was an interesting job. Pipes were in tight quarters. *(John fortunately never developed signs of asbestosis although some jokingly see evidence that the exposure affected his sense of humor.)*

Don Kelly, John's younger brother, who unknowingly caused John's trauma by being born, has fond feelings and memories of their childhood. Don says, "My three brothers and I grew up in the Haight Ashbury, or what is now called Cole Valley, in San Francisco, a block from Golden Gate Park and Kezar Stadium." Due to the proximity of the park Don says they spent untold hours recreating and playing ball "at the triangle and the little rec and big rec sites" in their free time.

During football season their weekends had the added excitement of selling programs at Kezar Stadium. On Sunday, Mass always came first, and the scramble to get to the Stadium afterwards added to the excitement. Their affiliation with Kezar Stadium extended when their dad, who was a ticket taker at the gate, "would sneak us into the games!"

Don recalls getting left behind on the occasion of the 1937 opening day of the Golden Gate Bridge. John and oldest brother Ray hiked out to attend the opening ceremony without Don.

Don said John excelled academically, and after eighth grade chose to enter the Minor Seminary at St. Joseph's College in Mountain View, forgoing a scholarship to St. Ignatius High School. St. Joseph's awarded students "premiums" (a variety of books) for excelling in their studies. "John would come home every June with an armful!" John graduated Maxima Cum Laude from St. Joseph's. The Dean of Studies told their parents that John could easily have graduated Summa Cum Laude, but unfortunately he was a bit too lazy in applying himself! John felt it always came too easily for him and he never felt challenged.

Don remembers that John played baseball for the semi-pro San Jose Orioles during vacation and during the school year he anchored the bass section of the seminary choir. Don says John still loves to sing and when given the opportunity he loves to break out in song.

Don calls John a gifted teacher who loved his roles as Dean of Students and as a teacher of Latin and English. He joined the lay faculty who went out on strike for higher wages against the Archdiocesan School Board. This required exceptional courage and conviction as he was the only priest faculty member to join the strike, much to the chagrin of the Diocesan Superintendent of Schools and some local pastors.

According to Don, all of this has carried over into John's years of work with the poor, the homeless, the hungry and the sick via Samaritan House, and currently with his Prison Ministry work at San Quentin.

(Don, tall like John but Scandinavian blond, followed John into the priesthood. He first completed St. Ignatius High School, then St. Joseph and St. Patrick's Seminary like John. Don was ordained a few years after John and served as a parish priest for a total of fifteen years. John said that "Don fell in love with a parish lady and left the priesthood around 1973.")

Two

Call To Be a Catholic Priest

John began his priesthood career at the mere age of thirteen, directly out of grammar school. You might ask, how and why would an eighth grader enter the seminary? In part it was related to the family structure as he got older. John said that his oldest brother Ray was an "absolute unbelievable renegade." By comparison, and in spite of his early difficulties with his mother, John became the good boy. His mother said over and over to him, "You're a good boy, Jacky."

John says he was encouraged by the nuns at St. Agnes Grammar school in San Francisco's Haight Ashbury district. The nuns thought he was cute, he was always at school helping them, and he was an altar boy. "I got totally engrossed in that whole church stuff." In those days nuns took a certain amount of pride in how many of the boys in their classes entered the seminary, and John thinks the nuns kept track of how many boys went on to study for the priesthood. At some point John became the "designated" future priest.

No visions or celestial appearances, no voices from above; John's call to the priesthood began in Catholic grammar school in the seventh grade. He remembers a parish priest visiting his class and asking if any of the boys had thought about becoming a priest. **Tom McMahon**, later a fellow seminarian, remembers **Butch Leonard**, a former WWII Marine Corps Chaplain, then a recruiter priest, making the case for entering the priesthood. And Tom notes that the early 1940s were the years immediately following the Great Depression. Tom says there were four kids on his block who entered the seminary and he believes that their dads probably said, "If you can get a secure job and three squares (meals) a day and a roof over your head – grab it."

John remembers thinking about it from seventh grade on and even praying for guidance from God regarding the possibility of a vocation. He said the recruiter priest wasn't pushy but did ask the class to think about it. The priest asked, "If you had been in church and had watched the priest and if that was something that you would be inclined to do, would you consider it?" John remembered when he was an altar boy being impressed with what the priest did. He was involved and was in the church all the time at the St. Agnes School. He could not get the thought out of his mind. This feeling of attraction lasted so he felt a responsibility to investigate it.

Right next to St. Agnes was a convent of nuns who had come from Mexico to escape persecution. In their convent they had a small side chapel with the consecrated host exposed full time for adoration. The nuns took turns praying in chapel and you could hear them in back. And almost every time John walked home from school he would drop in there. John thought, "I've got these feelings; tell me, Lord, if this is what you want. Give me some sign."

So in John's eighth grade the date was set for the test for entrance into the seminary. John took the test, found out he passed but was afraid to tell his parents that he had taken this momentous step. They hadn't known because he had done it entirely on his own. They eventually found out because one of John's eighth grade classmates told John's brother, "Hey, did you know your brother wants to go to the seminary?" So his brother rushed home and told their parents. John never had the courage to tell them. This was the summer of 1942 – wartime.

For John it was a combination of factors; with all that experience around church, it seemed like something he would like to do. At least that was the conscious part of it. There was also "the sneaky part of me that said, I'm not really making it in life the way I want. My older brother Ray is totally dominating the scene. When I get to high school he is going to be even more dominating. Going to the seminary was a way to get out of being dominated because it was respectable. Who knows how much that influenced my decision to become a priest?"

John began with faith mixed with doubts. He wondered at age thirteen if he had truly been chosen by God to be a priest. To slip from the shadow of his older brother, to be the success his mother sought and hopefully to please God, he entered the seminary.

Seminary Life for Young John
September 1942 was not yet a year after Pearl Harbor and the country's mood was fearful and uncertain. John hoped to find a safe harbor in the seminary. He may still have had doubts, but he was committed.

In John's day the Catholic Church's emphasis was to recruit boys right out of the eighth grade. Maybe they thought if they got them before they discovered sex .... Certainly it is true that 'as the twig is bent, so grows the tree.'

Along with fifty-five other pubescent high school freshmen, John left home and arrived at St. Joseph's College Seminary in Mountain View, California.

St. Joseph's provided four years of high school and two years of college. John describes the environment as monastic. He was separated from his family except for visits from one to four p.m. on the third Sunday of every month during summertime and a two-week Christmas vacation. His parents weren't allowed in the seminary building except for an entry parlor so they would park on the flat land outside and have a picnic. The bell rang at four o'clock, the parents left, the seminarians went back into their building, and "that was it." The rest of the time the boys did not see anybody from the outside. However, "During the course of the year my mom was extremely faithful and wrote to me at least once a week. My dad wasn't into that."

During summer vacation the students were expected to go to Mass every day but John says the seminary did not keep track of them. When they left in June they were given a topic to research and each got a turn to present their assigned subject when school began in fall. They were to spend two or three weeks of summer in community service such as a boys' camp or teaching catechism. John once taught catechism at Saints Peter and Paul parish in San Francisco's North Beach. He remembers a "hilarious" grammar school kid assembly with three hundred screaming Italian kids. John also counseled at Pop Philips boys' camp in Healdsburg.

Now, with his buddies at San Quentin, John compares prison life to seminary life – lots of kinship, structure and order and rooms no bigger than prison cells. The seminarians were not allowed to talk to each other at night. The black slacks and white shirt seminary uniform had even less color than the blue denim prison garb.

After six years at St. Joseph College in Mountain View, John attended St. Patrick's Seminary in Menlo Park, California for two more years of college and four years of theology. Today, kids first attend high school and only then enter St. Patrick's.

John did appreciate the camaraderie of the fifty-six high school freshmen at St. Joseph's but thought the academics were only adequate with some good and some horrible teachers. John was thought weird for his love of Latin and Greek *(Greek geek?)* while his classmates tolerated the subjects at best. The tradition was to use a "cheat-sheet pony" from an earlier class but John claims he always translated "from scratch." He thought if he was supposed to learn it, he would learn it and once gave a speech on "The Value of Greek in the Minor Seminary." His classmates thought he was a total nut, but John went on to teach Latin years later at Serra High School.

Seminary classes were Monday, Tuesday, Wednesday, Friday and Saturday and on those days students could not speak at dinner; rather, they listened to readings and speeches from a pulpit. They got excited when occasionally a visiting priest would share dinner with them and on those evenings they could talk in honor of the presence of the guest priest. John admits that they would sometimes call up a priest "to come visit so we would get a chance to talk." Students had Thursdays and Sundays off.

After breakfast they returned to their rooms only to make their beds. After study hall from seven-thirty to eight-thirty p.m. followed by night prayers they were allowed back to their rooms. Called the Great Silence, they were not to speak to anybody until breakfast the next morning *(sounds more stringent than San Quentin)*. John admits the rule was broken by students talking out their windows. John laughs about the common bathroom at the head of each stairway that was locked from nine to ten p.m. each evening, so if you had forgotten to go before lockdown and had to go during this time it was not unusual to see people "doing things out the windows." *(I didn't ask about John's personal experience.)*

The seminary dorm rooms were single occupancy and if you were caught in another person's room you were automatically expelled. That was one of the "fiercest rules of the seminary." Students were not allowed to socialize above the first (common area) floor. But John says that as a way to vent youthful energies students were intensely into sports. When a boy arrived at the seminary he was picked by the Ramblers, Trojans or Bears, each team captained by a sixth-year student. There were three different levels of intramural competition, one for each two-year group, and they kept track of who won. They also created a team that played semi-pro baseball scheduled during the summer weekends. John usually played left field but for a while he was a left-handed third baseman *(he says with a laugh)*.

In minor seminary they were allowed to walk to a local store and consume junk food and once per semester they were permitted to walk to the town of Los Altos. However they had to first sign up, be accompanied by a professor and were not allowed to hitch-hike. Some guys would hitch-hike but scrambled out of the car before they ran into the professor on duty.

Except for **Edna Bolling**, the seminary nurse, the only women on campus were an order of nuns from Canada who cooked the seminarians' meals, washed their clothes and kept the kitchen clean *(indentured servants?)*. Not allowed to talk to students, they mostly prayed and hid in the kitchen. Only nods in passing were allowed.

But fellow seminarian Tom McMahon recalled a "very robust" Mexican girl, Genevieve, working at St. Joseph's College when he was a junior in high school. The seminarians went to the office to buy a pencil. They'd make a subsequent trip to buy binder paper and yet another to buy other supplies. Tom said she lasted about six weeks before the faculty caught on and "kicked her out, I'm sure." Tom sums up the sexist seminary approach as "an ugly deprivation of maturity, manhood, adulthood." Tom says that **Richard Sipe**, a famous U.S. psychologist, has given a name to priests as "forever fourteen" – charging that guys in the seminary never had a chance to develop.

After six years at St. Joseph's John earned a BA degree in philosophy with a minor in Latin at St. Patrick's and continued there to complete four years of theology studies.

As an original classmate at "St. Joe's" and then at St. Patrick's seminaries, Tom McMahon was ordained with John. Only thirteen remained of their original fifty-six member class. Tom went on to be a priest for twenty-six years, "literally married with two kids *(not typical even during the priest shortage years)* in a parish way out in the boonies. Pretty soon the retired **Bishop Frank Quinn** rang the bell." Tom was at the parish of Community of Christ Our Lord and Brother in New Almaden, California. Tom, well known to be critical and outspoken, went to **Archbishop McGucken** and offered his resignation but was told to stay until another priest could be sent to take his place. Tom's few-months interim parish service turned into three years and didn't end until after Tom's second child had arrived.

Tom, recalling their seminary days, describes John as "smarter than some of the professors." In Greek studies "John never hurried in an exam and would never make a mistake." Tom thinks that John had little regard for the intelligence of the faculty and "there is no question that John excelled brilliantly in this educational system."

Tom also notes that seminarian kids conformed to the system without question. They conformed to the rules of dress, to the intellectual approach to studies, to a certain behavior "even when you went home." Tom said that on summer break "you were considered a junior priest" and were expected to conform to that image. "You were outside the realm of anything to do with women."

In day to day seminary life students were required to conform even to the athletic system. "Every kid had to participate or you would have gotten kicked out of the seminary." Tom says that "John was talented -- never a hot shot – but he enjoyed playing intramural softball, soccer, basketball, baseball, track and swimming." Tom describes the athletics as designed to "burn up the testosterone."

He added that seminary experience was "being watched for twelve years to see if you would be obedient. Any kid who was exceptional, who was different, would be dismissed." Tom tells how John and he would "break some of the rules. For two hundred dollars we bought and owned a sailboat that we kept down at Redwood City harbor. We were never supposed to sail unless we had three kids but we used to sail just the two of us." They left the boat behind when they were ordained and others took it over.

"Very cautiously we did things on our own." But there was a kind of "cloak of secrecy and seminarians typically did not know much about each other." Tom says, "You get blended in the beginning in the minor seminary and this is in preparation for your blending into the priesthood as an anonymous person. You are going to be a pastor, get moved around, so don't make too many friends; just do your job, be obedient and keep away from women. The object of the seminary was to make monks of the seminarians yet ask them to live in the real world."

John got "blended and conformed" enough to get through the twelve years. The first six years he says were easy because he was a "naive little kid" during high school at St. Joseph. John had been largely sheltered and isolated from his family and the turmoil and anxiety of the times. He described those minor-seminary high school years as "somewhat clueless" but nonetheless "relatively peaceful and pleasant."

His St. Patrick's years were much more difficult due to his "confused sexual feelings." He got so little information his first six years that he "didn't know what was going on. I didn't know what intercourse was until I was in college." When he began to realize his sexual feelings and was confronted by all the rules of the Church, he "felt that something was wrong with me." The sense of the priesthood that John grew up with was that you were supposed to get so holy that you were beyond sexual feelings. Just having forbidden thoughts was considered bad.

Experiencing creeping doubts, John asked himself, "How could I be having forbidden sexual feelings yet imagine I could become a holy priest?" He feared he would not or could not meet the spiritual expectations of Holy Mother Church and attain the esteemed and venerated office of priesthood.

But John pushed his doubts aside and pressed on to honor his original commitment to become a priest.

John Becomes a Priest

Catholic Holy Orders are a series of steps leading to becoming a priest. John explains this ordination schedule: "At the end of the second year of major seminary at St. Patrick's you begin the seven steps of Holy Orders and become eligible for the ceremony of Tonsure. This is your commitment to becoming a clergyman. At the end of the fourth year you become a Sub-Deacon, Deacon at the end of the fifth year, and Priest at the end of the sixth year."

John recalled issues with the Sub-Deacon ceremony, the major step of coming to grips with the vow of celibacy. With serious doubts about his commitment and on the day of the ceremony he actually backed out for a time. "It wasn't that I had the urge to get married. It is just that what I was feeling sexually didn't fit. I wanted to get to the place where I felt better inside. My feelings were bouncing me all over the countryside." John showed up ready to go through the ceremony but "panicked and got off the altar and left."

John struggled to decide what he wanted to do. But "I made the commitment to follow through the process of becoming a priest. I do a lot of things out of sheer will power – things that don't necessarily feel like they connect."

The Korean War started and ended while John was in major seminary and still the country and John felt uncertain. In this environment John was ordained with a cohort of about thirty-five others on Friday, June 11, 1954 at Old St. Mary's Cathedral in San Francisco. Even that day he "did not do a handstand. I think I told the guy next to me as we were all prostrate on the altar to grab me to make sure I don't run."

That night John and his folks went to Fisherman's Wharf for dinner. The following Sunday he said his first Mass "which was a big deal" and afterwards had a reception for family and friends. Then John gave everybody a blessing *(he laughs when he describes this)*. John says of that original ordination cohort: "One third still in; one third dead; and one third out."

John got a taste of Church politics observing two brothers in his class who had come from a wealthy Peninsula family. After ordination both were sent to major cities, one to Oakland and one to San Francisco "where they had many lucrative Mass stipends *(pay to pray?)*." In contrast, John was sent to Santa Rosa which then was a small young community. "There were no old people whatsoever and few Mass stipends."

John also recalls that a week before ordination the treasurer of St. Patrick's seminary called the seminarians in one by one and said, "How are you going to pay your back tuition that you were unable to pay during your twelve years here?" John had no idea this was coming. So those in the class who were poor (not the two Peninsula guys who obviously had paid up their tuition) had to take out a fifteen year life insurance policy, so if they died the seminary and the Archdiocese got paid back. It was mind boggling to John at the time.

After ordination, all recreation was now with John's fellow priests: golf on Wednesday and golf vacations to Monterey or Santa Cruz with three or four other priests. John now sees this as kind of strange.

Up to that point and for most of his following life it was about male companionship: male classmates in the seminary taught by male priests and instructors, all with little contact or understanding of the female of the species. "The last thing in the world we were given to understand was what sexuality was all about. The only thing I remember was negative. We were told that, as seminarians studying to be priests, we were special. If we committed a sexual act, it wasn't just a mortal sin, it was a sacrilege because we're sacred. *(How*

ice a mortal sin will already send you to hell.) They'd always tell us
.ere were different vocations in life – married or priesthood – and 'you
.inarians are in a separate category, way above everybody else.'"

The carryover for John is tough. "Not only do I not know how to relate
to women, but there is a part of me that was trained to be, I don't want to
say hateful, but to not trust women." The message they got was that women
would get them in trouble. "Even today I have a horrible time relating. I do it
externally and I do get along with women. But internally it still is a challenge
after all these years."

John's folks never talked about sex, he left home before he was fourteen
and then spent his whole time with boys. By the first or second year at St.
Patrick's he started feeling like "a dreadful sinner" because he had gone
through those years with thoughts he was not supposed to have. They were
supposed to have asbestos covers around them and these things were not
supposed to happen. John said that the only time that sexuality came up was
when they were studying moral theology and what constitutes a mortal sin.
Never did they discuss how they were to deal with it.

A series of books on religion in high school seminary contained two or
three pages about sexuality. The teacher told students to staple those pages
together and not to read them. They were not allowed to have an Old Testament
because there were a couple of sex stories in there. John notes that much of
the sexual stuff done by clergy reported in recent news was done by people
around his age cohort, all with a lack of sexual training.

After two years in a parish in San Francisco John was assigned to all-male
Serra High School. There he lived in a faculty house with twelve other priests.
"It was almost like women didn't belong in our world, like women were an
anathema; they were not part of my existence."

John later spent a year at the Graduate Theological Union in Berkeley
where a nun, **Jean Depauw**, was in some of John's classes. "We became
friends – nothing romantic at all. I think she may have wanted to be romantic
but I didn't." One day she was down on the San Francisco Peninsula and John
took her out to dinner. It turned out that John's folks' best friends were there
as well that night for dinner and John introduced her. The next time John
went home, his mother asked, "Are you leaving the priesthood?" John asked,
what? "Well, you were out with a lady." John says this shows how intense that
celibacy issue was.

Even today John feels uncomfortable having interactions with women. "It
makes no sense. It is so hard to explain." In some of the groups he's involved
in, some women become "very dominant and controlling in a sneaky way.
There are women who are sneaky aggressive, am I right?" And the trouble is

those are the ones "who are in my consciousness more than anybody else. It is very spooky."

John says that he and his fellow seminarians were trained "not really to be anti-feminist, but to pretend that women don't exist." In John's day "a woman wouldn't dare be on the faculty at Serra High School and would be looked upon with scorn if she tried to be involved."

It is interesting to think about vowing celibacy before ever having experienced anything else. John stated that he has never in his life experienced "romance."

I didn't have the nerve to ask John if he has remained celibate all his life. I did note that he is a 'hot item' in the senior center where he lives now; the ratio of women to men looked to be about five to one. I happened to pop in for a visit when a lady neighbor faked losing her cat and came calling on John in a transparent attempt to score some points. She stood no chance after she expressed a fervent desire to see all criminals locked up forever and a day. John has always been in favor of rehabilitation and restorative justice.

John was initially assigned to St. Eugene's in Santa Rosa shortly after ordination but only from June to August in 1954. John's predecessor priest had been the chaplain of a place called Los Guilicos juvenile detention facility just outside of Santa Rosa for the "worst teenage girls in the State of California." All of a sudden the Church administration decided that John was too young to be the chaplain there so they shipped him to San Francisco.

So John's actual first permanent assignment as a priest began when he arrived at the San Francisco parish of St. Emydius, 286 Ashton Avenue. Appropriately he is the patron saint for protection against earthquakes. This was the Ingleside neighborhood just off Ocean Avenue. In the olden days a rectory in San Francisco would have a pastor and at least two assistants and maybe another priest in residence but who worked elsewhere. And always the youngest priest was some guy recently ordained so his whole role was to take care of the parish teenagers and the kids. John oversaw a teen club and all kinds of activities like CYO (Catholic Youth Organization).

Those activities rarely happen now because there are so few priests around to do it. John had an eighty-year-old Irish pastor, **Father Motherway**, who liked John. John said they were "buddies." Number three in the pecking order, he began to learn about the vow of obedience. Twice the pastor did get mad at him: once for putting incense in the thurible, a metal censer, with the wrong hand and once for leaving early for a Forty-Niners game at Kezar Stadium and sticking the pastor with an afternoon baptism.

Initially John enjoyed this assignment because he spent his life there with kids. They had a gym which John would open on Sunday afternoon to play with the kindergarten through eighth grade kids. John said the parish had great families.

But John was young and newly minted as a cleric in his first parish job. With so little life experience he felt presumptuous blessing and advising a more mature congregation from the pulpit. Here he was not yet twenty-six years old telling people "what's going on spiritually." He asked himself how he could counsel on spiritual matters while he struggled with his own spirituality and commitment. In spite of his doubts, he liked the parishioners and had a lot of fun.

Hearing confessions was pretty routine but occasionally a little kid would come in and have no idea what he was doing and John would cue him with "bless me father...." That could be a bit frustrating. More of a challenge was on Christmas Eve and the Saturday before Easter when the once-or-twice-a-year folks would show up. Confessions were supposed to end at nine p.m. and he'd look out and still see twenty people in line.

At the end of his second year at St. Emydius John began to seriously doubt his fitness for the duties and rituals of parish life. He got to the point where he did not feel like saying Sunday Mass: "I didn't feel like I fit in that role." He'd get a visiting priest to say his assigned Mass and take off to the coast and just sit and look at the water. He began to think about leaving the priesthood because of his "intense internal conflict and confusion."

In the summer of 1956, just two years after ordination, he actually wrote a letter to his parents telling them he was heading to Canada and was going to hide. He kept the letter un-mailed for a very long time. He said he just had to get out of there. But about that time he received his notice of transfer to Serra Catholic Boys High School. John said something kept him from deciding to leave it all behind and made him want to at least look at what Serra was going to be like. John accepted the transfer and reported for his teaching assignment.

Three

Serra High School in San Mateo, California

It turned out that Serra fit perfectly. John found he didn't have to worry about the official things he had to do as a parish priest. And he got to interact with students whom he loved dearly. "It was fun, sheer joy. I would never have been a priest for twenty-five years if I hadn't gone to Serra High School."

Dissatisfaction with official church services led him to create "stuff that was different and not according to the rule book." He was the chaplain of the athletic team and whenever Serra had a football game he would say a Mass at nine a.m. He would preach a sermon that was a little out of the norm and get the kids involved. Afterwards they'd all go out to breakfast. It was a much freer activity than at a parish.

John's first year at Serra was 1956 and **Carl (Red) Moroney** was in John's freshman homeroom. Red grew up in San Mateo and after Serra High School went to Notre Dame University and USF Law School. He spent a year in Vietnam with the U.S. Marines and returned to practice law locally. Red has one son and three daughters and the son also graduated from Serra. John officiated at the son's wedding.

In addition to homeroom Red had John for a counselor "and we have been good friends ever since." At twenty-eight John was not much older than the students and "was a little apprehensive like they were -- the first day of high school." In those days, according to Red, John did not seem so focused on social justice the way he is now. But he was really into kids and sports. Red thinks a lot of it was that "he went into the seminary right out of grade school. This was his chance, in a sense, to go to a regular high school."

Red recalls that John was "just fantastic to us. He drove us to ball games." John did a lot of things that today you could never do. They went on overnight trips. They went down to Los Angeles to a state track meet. "He was like a big kid." He'd pile five or six of them into his car, initially a black Plymouth sedan. Within the first year he bought a station wagon so he could haul them all around. "And we'd drive him crazy. We'd be smoking in his car and he hated the smoke. It was crazy."

One weekend John gathered a bunch of guys together to go out and fix up the baseball field for the year. They did the raking and dragging and lining of the field. Red likes to think that they were volunteering but more likely "we were in trouble and this was part of the discipline." John had a big truck and loaded stuff to bring to the field. Red was standing up in the back of the truck as John turned into the school off Twentieth Avenue into the Serra driveway between two buildings. There was a connecting overhead archway and "I turned around just as we were going under the archway and it caught me right in the head. I was out cold and John was apparently panic stricken. So I never let him forget that he gave me a big scar on my hairline."

John was really into sports. He coached freshmen basketball and he'd take them all over to the games. "He was a good teacher but he was a tough teacher." Red took Latin for four years and for three of those years John taught it. "He was huge on Latin and Greek. In fact when they had to attend jug – after-school detention – there were always maybe fifty students in the library. John would make us write Latin the entire hour that we were there." He also taught English but Red didn't have him for English class.

Once Red didn't like a grade John gave him so "I started ignoring him. I didn't talk to him; I was just acting like a punk for a couple of weeks. I'd be kind of snippy with him if he'd ask me a question." So one time after a football practice John grabbed Red and pulled him into the tape (rehab) room. He started kind of side punching Red on the chest. "I'm tired of your attitude." Red says "he kind of scared me. Then we were OK. I straightened out and stopped acting like a jerk."

John Kelly acknowledges that he was strict. He enforced the dress code: no jeans, only shirts with a collar, leather shoes – no Keds or sandals. John sent improperly dressed kids home to change and then put them in detention after school. John said the dress rules applied to any school function, even football and basketball games. John would carry a notebook and write down the names of kids not properly dressed. On Monday morning he would get on the PA system and announce: "The following students will report to detention after school…" and he would list the names.

John worked over the freshmen and sophomores and established a reputation of being strict. Eventually the job became easy because "the fear was already in place." By the time the "disturbers" and "troublemakers" became seniors, they'd come up to talk to John on the school yard "because we were buddies."

Dolores Kelly-Hons and **Al Hons** describe John's discipline from the parents' point of view: Dolores (no relation) says when John was at Serra High School he was "the Dean of Boys and he was strict – really, really strict. Even the parents were frightened of him." Dolores married Al Hons after she was widowed and here is how Al remembers strict John: "I had seven kids, six boys, four who went to Serra. My (then) wife was just terrified when one of the kids was sick and she would have to call John and tell him that so and so wasn't going to be coming to school today. She would just break up and say, 'Why don't you call John.' She finally got over it a little bit but still was terrified that she had to call John Kelly, Dean of Boys."

John says as Dean of Students he had a dual philosophy: "I had to make sure they knew that I was in charge *(said with a certain amount of conviction)*. And acting as a human being I had to have them understand that I was their friend." John didn't think there were many Deans of Students driving students around town during leisure hours.

John said he had to make sure the students followed the regulations. "It's that simple." One time he looked up at the ceiling over the auditorium and saw 'fuck Kelly' written there. So he thought "OK, I'm a success." John says, "Teenagers, being what they are, you can treat them as kids who are a lot of fun but also there are kids with their own agendas who you have to control." John thinks the kids appreciated how they interacted. "Anytime we were at a bowl game, the kids and I were perfectly friendly."

John "spent fifteen years with teenagers who people think are horrible to deal with. But once a teenager thinks you are a good guy you are in business." John maintains that teens are like cats when you first meet them; they want to know, who *are* you and what are you *doing* here? But after they know you they are like dogs and want to be petted and shown attention. "There was not a single day that I did not enjoy walking into the Serra High School building."

John Horgan, now a well known local reporter, also began as a Serra freshman during John's first year. "Serra had some stellar individual athletes and John nurtured those young men." He once let some of them borrow his station wagon for a trip to Berkeley and as it entered the Treasure Island tunnel the vehicle emitted a loud backfire. They discovered that just because John was a Catholic priest, it didn't mean the heap had been maintained properly.

John loved winning, especially because Serra was just starting to flex its muscles as enrollment grew and its teams and their reputations got stronger. He was particularly pleased when Serra football, basketball and baseball teams defeated Jesuit rival Bellarmine Prep of San Jose. And John did whatever he could to facilitate those victories.

John Barrett, Serra Class of '69 and now a fellow San Mateo Rotarian, describes John as "tough but helpful. No nonsense old school. The big fist." Barrett acknowledges that he generally avoided teachers and especially stayed away from authority figures like the Dean of Students, John Kelly.

Gerry Bundy, also a Serra student and a fellow Rotarian, had this observation: "John Kelly had a really good hook-shot... as demonstrated during Senior/Faculty basketball games. He had an unparalleled advantage.

It was the pinky finger on his shooting hand, bent perpendicular to his other fingers at the hinge joint."

John's crooked pinky finger, for those who notice but are too polite to ask, was the result of a diving end-zone touchdown score during a touch football game at St. Patrick's Seminary. His finger was temporarily fixed but reverted its crooked position.

In September 1967 while still at Serra, John was sent by the San Francisco Catholic Archdiocese to Notre Dame University in South Bend, Indiana, to advance his study of Theology. John says that Notre Dame allowed him to be much more "hang-loose. I had nothing official to do. It allowed me to figure out what was going on." He was surprised when he heard of some of the new concepts that had come out of the theological world in the 1940s and 1950s that had not been introduced in the seminary. John and his fellow students had been taught traditionally throughout out their twelve years of training.

At Notre Dame University it also dawned on John that much modern interpretation of scripture and free-world theology had not been addressed in the seminary. John learned that the Bible was open to interpretation according to the culture in which it was written. It wasn't black and white, once-and-for-all, this is right and nothing else fits. It's like "the God force in this world and within the Church is developing; there is a spirit of openness to new things and growth." It is almost like the human race "has this world entrusted to it and you don't sit still with it – you keep learning new things all the time because new things are being discovered all the time."

John never experienced the conflict between science and theology since he sees science as "a gift of God to learn more and more about what this world is all about." To think there is a conflict between the two is ridiculous in John's humble opinion. "So at Notre Dame my whole thinking began to change dramatically."

This period also provided John with an unexpected opportunity to exercise his embryonic interest in social justice – in this case, the segregated South during the 1968 civil rights movement. John remembers staying in touch with five or six Serra graduates at Notre Dame. **Dan Johndrow** and others had been good friends of John's at Serra. One of them said, "Some of the (white) students here want to go to South Carolina on Easter vacation and register black voters and it would be great to have you go down with us."

John thought about it, and so with three or four of the Serra kids he went. They were there for only four or five days but those were "unbelievable days. Our headquarters became the house of the head of the NAACP in Hampton County, South Carolina. We actually slept there in his house – bunk style all over the place." NAACP had lined up some black kids to join the Notre Dame group and take them around to the places to register people.

John says that two of these kids, **Fast Eddie** and **Easy Eddie**, were about eighteen or nineteen years old. He "fell in love with both of them. They were two of the nicest kids I ever met in my life" and John regrets not having stayed in touch with them. "Two super kids. They'd take us around and show us where the people were and the team would go door to door and ask folks to register and get them to sign." John didn't remember any difficulties. The black neighborhoods were very neat and well kept but they were very isolated.

John remembers one day it was very warm and at noon they decided to stop and grab a drink and something to eat. The local kids got out of the car with John and walked into a store to sit and buy something. "And everybody, *everybody* stops, it was just like a freeze went on." They all seemed stunned that a white person was walking around with two black kids. John had never seen anything like it. It was like, what is going on that black kids are actually associating with white people?

One registration spot was five or six miles from where they were staying. As John was driving back that night a South Carolina Highway Patrolman got on his tail and followed him the whole way. "He seemed to be waiting for me to make a mistake." Then one of the Notre Dame students did get stopped and got a ticket. They all went to appeal and the judge was holding court in the back yard of his house. "The whole thing was a farce."

On Sunday morning the NAACP guy invited John to his Baptist church. "I said Mass in his front yard and I'm embarrassed to this day that I never invited the black people to receive Communion because I was still hung up on Catholic rules." John was invited to say a few words. "It was the first time I saw a congregation raising their arms and saying, Yay, Yay! And then when it came Communion time they asked me to be one of the ministers and I was so bloody embarrassed but it was just an amazing experience." Someone made a comment that they were very impressed with the blacks' togetherness and family structure and John said whatever you do, if you ever finally get liberated, "don't change the togetherness because this is beautiful."

On Monday night the black folks had a party in their little hall outside of town. Here were these white kids from Notre Dame dancing up a storm with all the black girls from South Carolina and John thought this probably had never happened here before.

A white couple who ran a local renegade newspaper was doing stories about them. They had written another story about some white people rabble rousing who had critically mentioned Senator Strom Thurmond's name – and suddenly they disappeared; nobody knows what happened. The Senator's critics just weren't around anymore.

John remembers that he called his mother on Easter night on a pay phone and didn't dare tell her where he was because "I'm not sure how my folks would have accepted it. It all was a fantastic experience – very eye opening."

(I happened to be in Navy flight training in Meridian, Mississippi in 1966 just before John was in South Carolina registering black voters. Following JFK's call for legislation in 1963 and then the passage of the Civil Rights Act of 1964 there was much discontent and resistance in the South. I copied and distributed to family an openly bigoted editorial of the Meridian Star newspaper that warned of miscegenation and mongrelization of the races (read white race) and vowed resistance to integration. South Carolina resisted as well and their elementary schools were not racially integrated completely until 1970. John was clearly on the social leading edge in 1967.)

John believes, especially from his earlier courses at NDU, that the whole purpose of being a Christian is to make a real difference in the world and not just talk about it. One weekend at Notre Dame John was asked to substitute by the pastor of a white parish in a minority black neighborhood in South Bend. John asked the pastor what he did to help those black minorities and was told that it was "none of our business – they are not Catholic."

The most important thing that came out of the experience at Notre Dame for John was "that no matter what else is going on, you need to be true to yourself and make sure that what you are thinking, saying and doing fits with who you are."

When Martin Luther King died, John was disappointed by Notre Dame's overall reaction. He and another priest went to downtown South Bend to the city's commemoration event and they discovered that Notre Dame had chosen not to be officially involved.

"All of these thoughts were accumulating and asking me, who are you and what do you want to do with yourself? I could see that the social issues I was interested in were not where I'd be able to spend time because of the Church's organizational structure."

Notre Dame had given John a taste of liberation theology and Vatican II, the Ecumenical Council. These new ideas along with the deep-south black voter registration drive changed John forever. He returned home in June 1968, just months after the Tet Offensive and during increasing public disenchantment with the Vietnam War.

John discovered a subculture of kids back at Serra who were disillusioned and sort of anti-jock. He connected and felt really at ease with them and promoted their cause. John once tried to get the Boosters Club to expand beyond their athletic focus and to promote arts and crafts – and "I got shot down. So I became something of a renegade."

It may have been a mistake to send an intelligent, thoughtful, truth-seeking priest to learn what was happening in the contemporary theology world. John learned, for example, that the Bible was never meant to be taken literally but was rather a collection of stories meant to teach a point. The point was important, not the literal language. It is ironic that John learned from a modern Catholic university the discrepancy between today's more fundamentalist, ritualistic Catholic Church and the simple Bible lessons of compassion and love. The Notre Dame mind-expansion experience added to his dissatisfaction with Church bureaucracy and got John wondering about his long-term career path.

Career Doubts

Soon after John returned to San Mateo from Notre Dame he was invited by the area Deanery (a San Francisco Archdiocese sub-region) to talk to his fellow priests about his Notre Dame experience. John gave them some ideas about new thinking in theology. When he finished the head of the Deanery said, "Well, this is all very nice but this has nothing to do with the Catholic Church." So John's message did not last. *(Liberal Theologians have never gone over well in the Catholic Church hierarchy.)*

Back at Serra he found his duties had a different feeling. He wanted to be sure that he was teaching and speaking and doing the *truth*. John says, "I believe we should bring the old along that still fits and change the old that doesn't fit and make it new."

Initially assigned to teach two or three religion classes, John said he couldn't do it. He told the understanding principal that he just didn't fit into that program and was granted a leave of absence. After a couple of months John taught Latin and ran some programs but did not again teach religion. John said that the traditional religion class approach no longer fit. He did more "out of class to help kids get engaged."

John saw the Catholic Church institution as stuck and "hung-up by tradition and image." The language of the liturgy and catechism were "not dealing with the real world. The Church wasn't taking in the progress from the old to the new." John says the Church, for example, didn't worry about racial integration because there were no or few minorities coming to the Catholic schools.

The wealthier people on the San Francisco Peninsula sent their mostly Catholic kids to private or Catholic schools. The battle then to break down the racial barriers was fierce. There was one kid at Serra who was half black and half white and John began to realize that a few black kids were beginning to come to Serra, but they were not the norm. John got to be friends with some of them and to see what it meant for them to be coming to Serra. A couple of the families just wanted their kids to get a better education. These kids had not been raised as Catholics, yet the other kids at Serra accepted them readily. The black kids left after school and went back into their culture which was like a different world.

Lynn Swann, the pro football player, was not a Catholic but had a lot a talent and became a highly respected student leader at Serra. **Billy Jackson**, as a senior in 1971, was asked what it was like to be at Serra. He said "during the day I'm here and it is fine with the guys. When we go home everybody else goes west and I go east."

After Notre Dame, John gradually got involved in race and integration issues which he didn't see the Church addressing. He joined the local Conference on Religion, Race and Social Concern which became the Interfaith Network for Community Health (INCH). The group was ecumenical and dealt with community issues, especially integration. John became increasingly involved and met with them every Wednesday morning at the A.M.E. Zion Church in San Mateo. The group included the black pastor at A.M.E., the pastor of St. Gregory's, a representative from the Protestant Church and **Rabbi Rosen**.

John began to recognize "a gap between what I thought Jesus was all about and what he expected us to do in the world versus what the Church was doing." His conflict grew as he observed this gap in his own community. He attended a Thanksgiving conference celebration that included people from all Christian denominations and other religions as well. A main topic of this conference was the historic late-1960's integration of the schools. But some Christian religious communities refused to participate because some funds from a collection were going to non-Christian causes.

While making many friends and influencing probably hundreds of folks – especially young folks – Serra became a maturing time for John. The initial challenge of teaching boys and participating in all manner of sports became not enough for him.

John's renegade career started in 1969 while he was still teaching at Serra High School. Some parishioners were up in arms about nearby St. Matthew's Grammar School deciding to hold their eighth grade picnic at the still segregated San Mateo Elks Club. Some parents of black eighth graders went to the principal but were unable to get the venue changed. The parents then went to the pastor and finally to the Archdiocese and no one would touch it.

Shortly thereafter on a Friday, a freshman student with a white mother and a black father put fliers in the faculty mail boxes. The fliers invited them to the King Community Center for a meeting that night. As this kid was putting the fliers in the boxes, the principal of Serra came and took a look at what was going on and said, "This is none of our business, take this stuff and get out of here right away." Hearing about the issue and how this student was treated made John furious and he spent the rest of the afternoon asking himself, "Do I or don't I go to King Center? So I went to the King Center." There they decided to picket St. Matthew's Church on Sunday during the Masses. So again John spent all day Saturday thinking, "Do I or don't I? Finally, I realize, I have to say the last two Masses, so I can't go, so I say the hell with it."

But after the early Mass John drove to St. Matthew's and was still debating whether he should or shouldn't join the protest. A couple of people who were at the meeting saw John so he thought, "I'm stuck now, so I went out. There I am standing in my Roman collar at St. Matthew's Catholic Church picketing this eighth grade picnic at the Elks Club." A number of good Catholic parents had kids at Serra and who belonged to the Elks Club. "They were not wild about seeing me."

*The Elks Lodges nationwide, including the San Mateo Elks, did not allow black members until the 1970s or women until the 1990s. In 1993, handball player and attorney **Angela Lim** sued the men-only San Mateo Elks Club for excluding her from an amateur tournament held there, arguing that the event was public even if the club was not. The case was settled out of court, and the club began to admit women in 1998.*

John was standing there at St. Matthew's and at first a number of people were happy to see him. Then they realized why he was there and suddenly the expressions on their faces changed dramatically. There was one guy in particular who had six or seven kids. He drove up with all his kids, realized why John was there, and flipped John the bird.

For John the St. Matthew's protest weekend was "part of the inner battle to protect myself and my image and to be honest and fair." John knew he didn't have to join the protest and that he'd still be OK if he didn't participate. But when he saw something wrong he had to do something about it. John felt that the Church position was outlandishly wrong and had to be challenged. Once he joined the protest, he said, "I felt no sense of conflict."

Tom McMahon reports that at this St. Matthew's protest, John, in clerical garb, was harassed by a parishioner for protecting the black students. Tom says that from that point on John was never the same and that his whole attitude toward the Church was: "Don't talk to me, I don't want to bother with those guys – I don't want to have anything to do with them." John agrees that this incident was the epitome of defining the disconnect between the Church institution and reality.

A couple of years after returning from Notre Dame John decided to leave the Serra faculty house. He ended up in residence at St. Mark's in Belmont while still teaching at Serra.

Another Straw Overloads the Camel

In the fall of 1971 there was a teachers' strike. The Catholic school system up until the late Sixties functioned with religious nuns, brothers and priests as faculty. When John taught at Serra High School there were almost thirty priests on staff. Tuition was only fifty dollars a month – since priests were "cheap labor and they didn't have to pay us anything. We had a pseudo salary and were guaranteed room and board. I think we were given maybe $100 a month when I first started. But we would get Mass stipends. People would ask you to say a Mass on behalf of one of their relatives, somebody who died. You were able to keep that money."

Times changed and with fewer clergy around to keep Catholic schools open they needed more and more lay people – called "lay helpers" by the superintendents.' Most would come right out of school as practice teachers and then leave for a better paying job in the public school system. In the mid-Sixties the Archdiocese developed a lay teacher contract and set a salary scale based upon public school salaries. In the late Sixties when the contracts came up for renewal the Archdiocese balked at keeping public school salary parity because of increasing costs. So at Archdiocese schools, including Serra, the lay teachers decided the negotiations were not working and voted to strike.

Throughout the diocese only a few clergy and a few less senior lay teachers at Serra went out on strike. John was the oldest in service of the few priests at Serra to strike so the Archdiocese labeled him the ringleader. A former Serra priest, who had since gone to work for the Archdiocese, called John and said, "OK, you have had your fun, now get back to work." John told him he just didn't understand and hung up. John described "being all over the place for six weeks until this strike got settled.

"The Catholic Church said beautiful things about justice but they didn't practice what they preached." In the midst of the strike the principal at Serra was "very difficult and extremely right wing-ish." He called one day and asked if the priests who were out on strike would like to have a meeting with parents to explain their position. So the parents and priests got together one night and suddenly the principal announced a priest gag order. One of John's supporters in the audience said, "We came to hear what the priests have to say and I want to hear what Father Kelly has to say." So John got up and started talking and didn't have two sentences out of his mouth when some other parent stood up and yelled, "Who do you think you are? You are supposed to teach our kids. Go back to work. What do you think this is?" So John got nowhere. He walked out afterwards and four ladies who used to be his friends cornered him against the wall, screaming at him for "ruining their kids' education and not doing his duty."

John didn't think twice about his participation in the strike. He felt the Archdiocese position was wrong and said, "I don't care who likes it or doesn't like it, I've got to state what I feel is right."

John disobeyed by challenging his fellow teachers and superiors. He incurred the wrath of parents, peers and parishioners. John admitted a "personal cost" but that it was easy to bear because the students were on his side. After the assembly at Serra where John was prevented from explaining his view, he invited the students to St. Mark's and "they were totally committed to the purpose of the strike."

The teachers finally got a settlement and some good came out of the strike. They got a benefit package and tenure. The Archdiocese finally realized that Serra and their other schools were going to be run by lay people and that if you want quality teachers you have to give them something worthwhile. Since then things have changed dramatically. John thinks Serra now has a part-time chaplain and no priests on the faculty at all.

During this event John was gradually deciding to leave Serra and forming in his head the idea that if he continued to be a priest "I would become a rabble rouser about issues of justice where I felt that the institution wasn't following up on the beautiful stuff they say." He describes a gradual process. At the very end of that 1972 school year Serra had a faculty meeting that was supposed to be a little celebration. But there was never any real harmony after that Serra strike and the opposing sides never really got back together. The discussion topic at this meeting was next year's dress code. John put his hand up and said, "Considering all the wonderful things that have happened this year, I am very, very impressed that the most important topic for next year is what the dress code should be."

Along with an employment contract, the Archdiocese did develop a council of teachers who addressed the administration's needs. And the school developed a parent group to advise on school issues.

All of this was just another step in John's realization that his position as a priest was outside the norm. "I was very proud of myself for joining the strike and I knew then and I know now that I felt very, very right."

John leaves Serra High School

John says it was "a real struggle leaving teaching at Serra High School in 1972, like leaving a womb." In the fall of 1973, John went across the Bay to the Graduate Theological Union (GTU) in Berkeley for a year. He roomed for six months in the city of Pinole, California with a pastor and fellow student and then moved to an apartment in the nearby city of Concord. In June 1974 he graduated with a Master's degree in Psychology. John says that one of the few things he got out of the Church was tuition for both Notre Dame and GTU. He had told the Archbishop he was going for the degree in psychology because he wanted to return to downtown San Mateo to counsel in an office that housed the Council on Religion, Grace and Social Concern. Their object was to get religious communities to support social causes.

In spite of the earlier conversation, when John got back in June 1974 he received a letter from the Archbishop appointing him to a parish in Marin County. John responded to the letter by calling the Archbishop and reminding him of the prior conversation and their agreement that he would not take a parish assignment when he got back – so he just didn't go. John remembers that the Archdiocese used to print an official directory every year for priests and that year he wasn't listed. "I was missing in action."

Tom McMahon, John's seminary buddy, empathizes with John and calls him "the Jesus servant priest. He had a sense of service to Jesus, rather than a liturgical sense of putting on the priestly robes." Tom calls John Kelly "one of the most noble men I've ever met. He knows what his truths and values are. He is tremendously sympathetic and understanding of human nature."

After refusing the Marin assignment, John returned to St. Mark's Parish in Belmont, continuing to share a residence with **Pastor Dave Walsh** (whose brother Larry married and left the priesthood). John says Father Walsh was good to him and let him do what he wanted. John worked at the parish on Sunday and weekends but didn't have any official Church assignment.

John left Serra in 1972 but continued his St. Mark's weekend duties and remained a priest until 1979. During this time John officiated at many weddings and funerals and along the way made some lifelong friends. **Pam Frisella, Mayor of Foster City, California** is one of those friends and she tells her story of meeting John:

"New Year's Day 1977, my husband Danny, a 1963 Serra High School graduate, died in a dune buggy accident. We were living in Arizona at spring training where he was playing for the Milwaukee Brewers; our son was three years old at the time. My husband went out on a dune buggy and didn't come back. So after his death we came back to San Mateo because I had met Danny Frisella here on a blind date in 1970. We only lived here one winter in the six years that we were married but I decided I wanted to bring him back here for his funeral. So here I was thirty years old and seven months pregnant. People called me and said that Danny would want Father Kelly to do the funeral. I had never heard of Father Kelly. So I met John when he walked into the funeral home. He walked in with his Roman collar and was a nice looking man, maybe fifty years old then.

"The homily he gave at my husband's funeral made it sound like Danny was going to go to this fabulous beyond. He shared the story that when Danny was his pupil he would always be able to get John off track. Whatever they were supposed to be studying at the time, Danny would bring up spirit week or something fun and then John could not bring the class back. John said Danny was a person who had lived life and died the way he lived – having fun in a dune buggy. John consoled me during probably the worst days of my life."

Pam wanted to donate their friends' contribution money in memory of Danny for scholarships, and the Serra bureaucracy wanted to paint the gym. So they collected about a hundred dollars to redo the athletic field and it became a community endeavor; every weekend for that entire summer they rebuilt that field. **Mike Peterson** was in his first year as principal, knew John and helped dedicate the field (Danny Frisella Memorial Stadium).

After the funeral John came over to Pam's sister's house where Pam was living until she found a house to buy. He would come over, not in his Roman collar – just a regular shirt, as a regular person. And he said, "Pam, even though you are not a Catholic, if you feel like you would want to come to St. Mark's Church in Belmont and take communion, by all means do it." Lutherans never had a problem with communion – you didn't have to sign a paper to go to communion. So she did and, through John, Pam met the Bradys, Tommy Brady's parents. **Galynn Brady** was pregnant and she came to the hospital to visit when Pam had Daniel three months later on her late husband Danny's thirty-first birthday. Through tears Pam remembers that "John was there with me all the way, bringing me a sense of peace. I just remember it so well – that sense of peace and hope that there was to be more to life. John brought me back from: I don't know how I am going to do this, to: I'm just going to do it. And there was never a doubt after that that I was going to be able to get on with my life."

So John became Pam's mentor. And when Pam went to the obstetrician the day after the funeral, she felt a strong bond with the doctor's nurse. Her name was **Janet Jones**, and Janet went home that night and called her really dear friend to tell him about Pam. And who did she call, but John Kelly. John and Janet suggested a three day retreat called Cursillo, and said they thought it would be really good for Pam. It was held at St. Benedict's in San Francisco and it was a distillation of a short course in Christianity.

Cursillo is the original three day movement and has since been licensed for use by several mainline Christian denominations, some of which have retained the trademarked "Cursillo" name while others have modified its talks and methods and given it a different name.

The Cursillo focuses on showing Christian lay people how to become effective leaders over the course of a three-day weekend. The weekend includes fifteen talks, some given by priests and some by lay people. The major emphasis of the weekend is to ask participants to take what they have learned back into the world, on what they call the «fourth day». The method stresses personal spiritual development, as accelerated by weekly group reunions (after the weekend). (Wikipedia.org, June 8, 2013)

In September, 1977, she left baby Daniel with a sitter and went on the Cursillo retreat. Janet was there and John was the spiritual director. Pam says, "That was the life changer for me. It made me realize it's not about me, it's about how I fit into this world and the connection with people and with my faith. The retreat was probably the single most important way that my life changed. I learned that if you look in the mirror you know that even if you are loved by no one else you are loved by God.

"So if John hadn't come into my life that day, where I would be or what I would be doing? It all came down, to there are no coincidences. There is fate and a direction and a path that I am on and if I had not run into John and Janet I don't know what path or direction I would have taken."

Pam is still Lutheran but her son Daniel was baptized by John in the Catholic Church because her late husband was Catholic. (Newborn Danny and newborn Tommy Brady were baptized by John together at the Brady house. They later played football together at Serra High School.) Then in 2007 John performed Daniel's wedding. Pam claims that everybody on the Peninsula has a John Kelly story: "He baptized our kids; he officiated at our marriage; he was there for my mother's funeral."

Four

John Turns in his Collar

John insists he didn't start out to be some sort of do-gooder in the community; "It just sort of happened." But he became more aware in the Seventies when he was still a priest that there was a gap between what the institutional Church was *saying* and what it was they *did*.

John just got more and more involved in local activities outside of officialdom throughout the Seventies. "I got to the point where I decided there were so many things going on in the Church that just didn't fit who I was." The social concerns group John worked with, for example, had a hard time getting clergy involved. "But the lay people were different. We had a group that met almost weekly and it was almost all lay people. The clergy were getting left behind."

John's transition time was primarily 1974 to 1979 while serving as a priest at St. Mark's Church in Belmont. Dolores Kelly-Hons was church secretary at the time and described John as the "supply" priest who worked outside at St. Mark's parish while initially still teaching at Serra High School. This out-of-the-way church was first housed in a general-purpose warehouse on Old County Road up against the railroad tracks. John started by changing Sunday around dramatically. "We did our own thing. We used the basic structure but we rewrote a lot of the liturgy according to weekly themes and brought in secular readings as well as scripture readings. We had a fantastic singing group singing non-standard music – standing room only on Sundays. The place was jammed. But it wasn't really official 'Catholic.' The pastor wasn't really into it but he let me do it."

However, a small nucleus of St. Mark's parishioners said that they were having a hard time because they thought John was breaking all the rules about how Church service and worship was supposed to be done. John said that the pastor called him in one day and suggested having a Mass on Saturday afternoon or Sunday evening where you do all these "shenanigans and have regular masses be official." So no matter how much John was able to draw people in with the new changes, some old-school folks were not pleased. "We had amazing things go on every Sunday. After Mass a whole group of people would go over to Hillsdale shopping center to have coffee and brunch together. It was a celebration." Many folks who had picketed discrimination at St. Matthew's had followed John over to St. Mark's.

During John's early years at St. Mark's when he continued to teach at

Serra, Dolores' oldest son **Brian Kelly** (later San Mateo Fire Chief) was a student and John often came over for dinner with **Father Dave.** Dolores said that John became just part of the family. He came to all the family affairs and got lessons in family dynamics. The kids were raised with him and loved him and John had a great time with them.

Dolores' son Brian got married in 1973 and they had a rehearsal dinner at the house. John was there because he was going to officiate at the ceremony. Many Serra guys were there who were going to be in the wedding party. After dinner they decided to take Brian out for a drink. **Chick Kelly**, Brian's dad, said he and John were going along. They went to the Fog Cutter bar in Burlingame. Somebody bought fourteen shots of Wild Turkey and set them up on the bar for Brian to drink. Chick said no, they would all share the shots. John had his shot of Wild Turkey and another and maybe another.

The next afternoon John officiated at the ceremony and his hands shook like crazy. John announced, "I'm shaking today but it isn't because I'm nervous. I'm hung over. The Kellys have taken me on the wrong path." John claims that that was the turning point for him to eventually stop drinking.

John tells about his folks' fiftieth wedding anniversary celebration while he was at St. Mark's. John wrote a Mass for them from beginning to end that was "nowhere in the book." A number of priests who were friends of John's family came and the following Monday John got a call from the Archdiocese bishop's office. The Archbishop's secretary came down to St. Mark's and said, "What right did you have to change the Mass around? You left this out. You left that out." So John asked him, "Did you look around to see if people were enjoying this experience?" His answer was, "That's beside the point!"

Dolores recalls John's transition from priest to non-priest. Vatican II was going on at the time and John was happy with those changes. He got involved with a group at St. Mark's and started a guitar-singing group and those same folks have been his friends for many years. Vatican II changed his whole attitude. She says that John "had so much talent; he is so smart. And that is why he has progressed as well as he has. He looked deeper into his feelings." She said that he tried to fathom why he wanted to change. Another person might just have gone along. With his intelligence, "he was looking for answers. And he found them."

During those years at St. Marks, Dolores saw the seed of the future Samaritan House started at Thanksgiving. The parishioners prepared boxes for people who needed assistance. From that group at St. Mark's John started another group at a San Mateo office where there were eighty people filling boxes. It began with maybe thirty families and then there were eighty. Dolores says, "It is amazing how it all developed."

Then when her husband died, John was there supporting Dolores and their family and was right there along with them for most of their baptisms, marriages and funerals. "He supported me and helped me bury Chick in 1977." She also supported John in his transition. They have been friends ever since. "John is a friend in word and deed."

Red Moroney and family had started attending church at St. Mark's in Belmont when Red found out that John had gone there after he left Serra. "It was a great parish and the Pastor there kind of gave John free rein. To some people in the church John's approach was considered a little bit radical. But it was really a wonderful, forward-looking parish – liberal in both the political and religious respect. John really drew a lot of people to the parish. People came from far and wide."

Red's family had a funeral at St. Mark's. They had a Down's syndrome child who also had a bad heart and at two months, as soon as she got sick, she died. John gave a sermon and presided at the funeral at St. Mark's. "It was unbelievable how John was able to talk about how much this two-month-old child had gotten out of life. It was so moving how he brought meaning to this little baby's life by talking about her mother taking care of her and feeding her, and the family gathering around her. It kind of made her sound like she had had a full life in just two months. It was one of the most unbelievable funeral talks I have ever heard. John has been a wonderful friend."

Red Moroney remembers when John threw a twenty-five year anniversary party for himself a couple of months before he left the priesthood. John wanted to get the party in before he departed. John said everybody sort of knew that he had had it with the priesthood. The party was held at St. Mark's in a big banquet hall with all kinds of family and friends. The community held that 'roast' for John and a short time later he left the Church.

Red thinks John left because he had "trouble operating within the bureaucracy of the Church." John became disillusioned and just felt it was time to do something else. It was shocking in a way and not shocking in another way. By that time John had become extremely active in social justice issues. He was concerned about the poor and about prisoners – the disadvantaged and the disenfranchised. It's not that he didn't always have those feelings, but at that time he became really active. As time went on "he became more and more interested in social justice and I think that is a lot of the reason that he left the priesthood."

Pam Frisella said that they were in a St. Mark's support group, again with Janet Jones along with three other couples. "We met maybe every other Sunday night. The big topic of conversation was that John was not happy. The bureaucracy of the Catholic Church was stifling John – he lost his glow, his ability to touch people." He could not do what he needed to do. Once John had stood up to the Catholic Church at the St. Matthew's discrimination protest, he and they knew he would continue to fight for what he believed. So the discussion question always was, what is he going to do? "Finally one night after six or eight months of, 'Should I or shouldn't I?', Janet Jones says, 'John, shit or get off the pot.' I'll never forget – it was priceless – that she called it like it was."

Tom McMahon told that story of John finishing Mass at St. Mark's and removing and dropping his cassock while singing 'Born Free.' Tom says, "This is the real John Kelly, the first time he really comes out in the open. The parishioners loved John's actions."

Tom says some "27,500 priests left the Church during the period of the 1970s. Everybody says, to get married. Not necessarily. Most of them left in disgust for what was happening inside the Church – the real wickedness, I call it. Most left because they were being honest – they weren't quitting anything. Then many of them had to live with someone and so they married."

After John effectively left the priesthood and St. Mark's, Serra principal Mike Peterson allowed John to use a little room in one of the school buildings. "Mike let me move in there just to have a place to crash so I could get away from everything and I stayed for probably a year. After that the Archbishop said, 'Well, why don't you take a leave of absence with pay.' I knew I wasn't going to come back but I got that minimum monthly stipend – maybe a hundred bucks – nothing to get excited about."

The year was 1979. Pope John Paul II visited Poland leading to the Solidarity movement and later visited the United States. Iran turned fundamentalist Muslim and took American hostages. Mother Teresa of Calcutta was awarded the Nobel Peace Prize for humanitarian work. And John Kelly left the priesthood wondering how he would advocate for social justice. And, by the way, how would he feed himself.

John moved to the little room at Serra High School, with no job, not knowing what the heck he would do. He survived only on his stipend and a little bit from counseling. He got his last stipend check in August 1980 with an official document. "I felt really hopeless; extremely hopeless. All of my identity for years went down the drain. I didn't know who I was from a load of hay." At that time John's brother was a prominent architect in San Francisco and they met at his office. When John walked in his brother said, "You just walked in like you are the weakest human being – like you are hopeless." For a long time John said he felt "really weird."

As soon as John left the priesthood the number of people who stayed in touch with him dwindled dramatically. He saw it as an indication of how important the imagery of clergy is for a lot of people. Some believe they have an inside spiritual or social track if they have a clergy friend. "I got some counseling here and there because I was experiencing real rage. All of the feelings I had been stuffing came out. I was angry as hell because of all that I had denied as being part of me. I tell people that in 1979 I was a fifty-one year old teenager who didn't know what in the world was going on, what I was going to do to survive."

Parishioner and friend **Jerry Forbes** said that he and his wife went through some of these issues with John. When he left the priesthood John thought that a lot of people were mad at him and, "probably we were. I think John went through a hard time after leaving the priesthood, asking who was on his side and who was not? We didn't see him for a while, not at Mass or church events. But after a time we got back together. Cursillo may have been a turning point."

Pam Frisella said unfortunately John did not go about leaving "in the proper way." And that really made people unhappy. She says that there must be a black list somewhere up in the San Francisco Archdiocese that says "do not talk to this man because he did not go through the right channels." He just quit. Maybe John remembers it differently, but later when he went back to Serra they were thinking of hiring him to teach. But the day he went to sign the employment papers the call came down: "Is that *the* John Kelly, the former priest? No, no you cannot hire him."

Pam said it was very cool that they had this friendship with the support group. He felt comfortable talking about this with the group because who else would he have been able to talk with about it? She remembers his retirement party at St. Mark's and that people were gracious. But she remembers distinctly that afterwards there was a fall-off of those Catholics who only wanted to associate with *Father* John Kelly. "There was a lot of hurt in John that I don't know how many other people have recognized. It didn't mean jack to me that John was a priest. He was just my friend." All the people who wanted him at their dinner table as a Catholic priest and a valued guest didn't want him anymore. So his social life went down the toilet and people just weren't calling him anymore.

John says that at this point he really didn't have a sense of identity. His whole self had been wrapped up in his priest identity. Even though he had not been a conventional priest, still, being a priest had been his identity. "All of a sudden I didn't know who I was. As a priest I didn't have to worry about my share of adulation. It came merely because I was a priest." John has since advised younger priests not to give up their identity and independence. But he allows that to some degree to be a priest you have to "sell your soul" to the organization of the Church. John looks now at the guys his age who remained priests and says it's hard to imagine them having a sense of "being anybody." John says you identify so thoroughly with the role of priest that it becomes your existence. The ability to maintain a broader vision of reality is a real challenge. The priesthood becomes the source of all your attention and positive reinforcement.

So John asked himself, where does he go with this new path? What he was going to do for a living? Nobody stepped up to offer John a job until he got that "wacky job as a courier." He wondered, "Should I live my life comfortably or should I get involved in something meaningful?" About that time, **Sylvester Hodges** twisted his arm to run a dining hall venture at King Community Center. "That sort of turned it around and gave me a base out of which to operate."

John has some historic heroes like Martin Luther King and Gandhi whom he credits with helping get him past anger and violence. John paraphrases one of Gandhi's "profound" statements: I will not make anybody my enemy; no matter how different I may be, or how opposed I am to what they are doing, there is something about them I can connect with. Having those larger-than-life mentors, along with being a priest and leaving the priesthood, helped John understand what Jesus was all about: "…don't get caught up with goods and property. Help people and forgive."

While John was in India on a retreat, the guy running it explained that people from India and the East look at the United States religious communities as "all show and no go; just window dressing." John says there is a lot of truth to that. "The things I ended up doing, I never could have done if I had stayed attached to the Church institution. Because of so many regulations and so much bureaucracy they could not get permission to do anything. "I just got tired of nothing happening on a concrete level."

During his career transition John tried attending a few churches in the area and went up to Glide Memorial Church in San Francisco but never found anything that fit. Once in a while he pops into church on Sunday. But now he has been involved with Kairos at San Quentin just about every Sunday for nearly fifteen years.

Starting Over Career-wise
John's degree in psychology from GTU and his training in psychology gave him one of his few marketable job skills. John had met some guys at a Cursillo spiritual retreat who ran a counseling office in Belmont. They let him use part of their office space to set up a small counseling practice to counsel a few people.

In the mid-Seventies John had passed the written test for a Marriage, Family and Child Counselor license. An MFCC therapist is one who has earned a Master of Science degree in counseling with a specialization in marriage, family and child issues. The year John took the test was the first year that the state had reinstituted oral exams. John sat before three or four people who were his oral examiners and barely got into the discussion when a woman examiner said to him, "You're obviously depressed, what do you do with your depression?" John looked at her and said, "Ma'am, I don't know where you are coming from but what has that got to do with what we are doing here?" John had had some real experience in counseling families, but not a lot. On the form they sent back to him, each one of the examiners had rated him in different areas. John noticed rating numbers that had been crossed out, convincing him that the woman examiner had railroaded him. "They knew I was a priest. So I got turned down. I flunked the oral so I never got the license." (Friend Tom McMahon says John flunked "because he was too damned honest.") John took it again later on but by then he didn't want to do it anyway. After it was all said and done John was convinced that he was a good counselor.

John still had friends but no job, few marketable skills and no source of income. One friend, **Tom Brady, Senior**, knew a guy who was running a company in San Mateo and got John a job as a courier delivering documents in the East Bay. Starting in 1982 he ran messages around from six o'clock in the morning until around eleven.

Pam Frisella asked, what does being a priest qualify you to do in the secular world? John did teach part time at Menlo Atherton High School and he did do family counseling for a while for a non-profit. She said he got into an accident while driving as a courier and the other driver was killed. "I think that changed his life and sent it into another direction. What a waste of his talent that he was sitting in that stupid car driving as a courier." After that maybe he had time to reflect. Maybe he had survivor guilt. "For me too; sometimes when you survive and somebody else didn't you need to just accept…." Pam said that's when John got involved with Samaritan House volunteering. Pam was then in the middle of raising children so they talked and saw each other only now and again.

John said he was working that courier job "just to pay my bills. I didn't know where I was going with any of it.

"On March 24, 1983 I was doing my job and driving over the hill on I-580 to Pleasanton and it was raining like hell and my car hydroplaned. I had no control and it crossed the double divide and I was hit by oncoming traffic coming up the hill. March 24, I'll never forget each year when it comes – the guy in the other car got killed." John ended up in the hospital with "nothing really major, I had wrecked a vertebrae and damaged nerves but didn't break anything." For John it was an "unbelievably traumatic experience." John was on disability for a number of months and got unemployment insurance. He said he "barely survived."

For John it was a very significant trial period trying to figure out who he was and what was going on. "And having this guy get killed was.... There is a line from Cursillo: There is no such thing as an accident. So here I am wondering, what does that mean? How does this happen? What did I do wrong? Oh, God, it was a real traumatic experience." John agonized over whether or not to make contact with the family of the guy he killed. John talked to some people and decided not to and he never has. "So I don't know what they think of me." It turned out that he was a fifty-one year old guy who had a couple of kids and they sued the company. That's how that chapter ended for John.

By the time of the accident John had moved out of his room at Serra High School and was living in an apartment on Hayward Avenue near downtown San Mateo. The building had been sold and the new owner raised the rents "unbelievably," so John moved to an upstairs unit in a house in Burlingame where he lived for twenty years. He had met a lady through counseling who knew the owners **Don and Barbara Athey**, an older couple, who gave John a substantial break on the rent. John's recent stroke forced him to finally give up the apartment since he could no longer negotiate the long, steep stairs.

This whole difficult transition for John, including the accident and move, was followed by an opportunity for which John Kelly is best known: the organization providentially called Samaritan House.

Five

Samaritan House, Feeding the Hungry

Jesus, some two thousand years ago, told a story to his Jewish listeners who typically held their Samaritan neighbors in low regard. As described in the Gospel of Luke, a lawyer stood up and tested Jesus, saying, "Teacher, how do I get to heaven?"

Jesus asked him, "You know the law. What does it say?"

The lawyer answered, "You shall love the Lord your God with all your heart, with all your soul, with all your strength, and with all your mind; and your neighbor as yourself."

Jesus responded, "You have answered correctly. Do this, and you will live."

But the lawyer, desiring to justify himself, asked Jesus, "So, who is my neighbor?"

Jesus answered with a story of a man traveling from Jerusalem to Jericho who was mugged by robbers. They stripped him, beat him and fled, leaving him half dead. By chance a Jewish priest came that way. He saw the victim, and passed him by. A Levite came to the same place, saw the man, and also passed him by. But a certain Samaritan, as he traveled, came to the victim, was moved by compassion and patched up his wounds with oil and wine. He loaded the man on his donkey, brought him to an inn, and took care of him. On the next day, before he left, he gave money to the inn manager, and told him, "Take care of this poor guy. If it costs more, I will reimburse you on my way back."

Jesus asked the lawyer, "Which of these three men was a neighbor to the guy who got mugged?"

The lawyer said, "The man who showed mercy on the victim."

Then Jesus said to him, "Go and do likewise."

Feeding the Hungry

John makes it sound like he was roped into the leadership of Samaritan House. Rather it was a marriage of convenience. John was divorced from his role as priest but continued to feel the call to help people in need. Sylvester Hodges made the first proposal to merely provide meals for the hungry folks in a poor area of San Mateo, California.

Sylvester was director of the King Community Center in San Mateo's North Central minority neighborhood. He wanted to start a dining room because many of his people "didn't get fed very well." Sylvester invited

John to come and be part of the planning and then to organize and lead the program. John became the director of that dining room program called INCH (Interfaith Network for Community Health) Hospitality Family Kitchen, and on April 11, 1984, John and his team served the first meal at King Center to thirty-two hungry people. They set up a kitchen and starting serving dinner two nights a week with their first food coming from St. Anthony's Dining Room in Menlo Park.

At that time a little referral agency called Samaritan House was located nearby and was run by three community workers supported by the City of San Mateo. They shared space with the Salvation Army and others. The County of San Mateo had a 'core' network of agencies throughout their jurisdiction except for Central County. In the summer of 1985, **Bonnie Bowling** and another County staffer invited John to help merge the King Center dining room with the small Samaritan House referral service to fill their service gap.

This time Sylvester Hodges from King Center headed the search to find someone to lead and implement this new 'core' concept. The committee sought a high-energy person with vision, commitment to move forward, and with community contacts; and who was willing to work for peanuts. Fortunately, John missed the meeting that resulted in a list of a half-dozen prospects but no prospect fulfilled the requirements. Suddenly Sylvester said, "We have been looking at the forest for a tree and we have the best tree right in our own yard." The committee all knew exactly who he had in mind. They anticipated John would say no, so they put together a convincing plan and voted in favor at that same meeting. At the next meeting, when John arrived they explained how hard the committee had worked on the criteria and selection of candidates. Sylvester said, "John complimented us and asked about whom we had chosen. I, as President told him how excited and confident we were in our choice and that *he* had been selected unanimously." As expected, John attempted to convince them to look for someone else but they convinced him to take the position on a trial basis and that was all it took. Sylvester said that John's successful tenure with Samaritan House proved the committee "picked the right person for the job."

The three original City-paid community workers were joined by a County-paid fourth to all work the new central area. John became director of the County core agency Samaritan House but **Hope Whipple Williams,** who now runs the San Mateo City Senior Center, initially supervised the three city employees.

Hope says she admires John who was *Father* Kelly when they first met. She recalled that the North Central Neighborhood Community would make holiday baskets for their less fortunate members. John provided his office as a location to prepare the baskets and as his counselees were waiting they joined in prepping the baskets. They had so much fun they asked if they could deliver baskets to some of the needy families. John had a way of attracting and energizing volunteers.

As the new Samaritan House director John had a primitive little office in the back of the Turnbull Elementary School gym (now College Park Elementary School), part of the San Mateo/Foster City Elementary school district. However, overcrowding soon prompted them to set up a portable building at the corner of Humboldt and Indian Streets which became the first official home of Samaritan House.

Sue Lempert is a former San Mateo Mayor and former Board member in various school districts. She writes a column for the San Mateo Daily Journal and has long been active with the League of Women Voters. Sue first met John while working for the non-profit Human Investment Project (HIP). Sue said John came to her Age Center Alliance and to other non-profits offering to serve the really underserved through Samaritan House. They all were happy to see him do this. They saw first-hand the pockets of hungry poor in the County.

John too soon discovered that hunger was not confined to the area around the King Center. **Evelyn Taylor**, principal of North Shoreview Elementary School, said that they also had families on the east side of town with no meals for their kids. So later in 1984 Samaritan House started serving meals at her school and within a couple of years they were doing meals five nights a week. There was no way to describe Evelyn, according to John. "She was amazing. She would not let any kids into her school unless the parents would sign a contract that they would spend a certain amount of time volunteering or actually spend time at the school. She had so many great things going."

Evelyn Taylor deserves her own biography for her pioneering work in the San Mateo/Foster City School system as an educator, administrator and member and President of the Board of Trustees. She was a tireless advocate for students and residents, especially of San Mateo's minority community. See: http://archives.smdailyjournal.com/article_preview.php?id=144839

She was a major influence on John Kelly's life and on the success of Samaritan House.

John recalls that St. Anthony's in Menlo Park committed to provide meals for their dining room for six months for free. Then they had to start paying for meals. So every day they sent a volunteer down to Menlo Park to get food and bring it to San Mateo. It worked but he said he knew that they couldn't use that model forever. Some five years later in 1989 they added a second mobile building to the Turnbull School campus to create a new kitchen. John attracted talent from his Board and knew a restaurateur who set up the kitchen equipment. "This guy and my Board volunteers knew what they were doing. It was all just a fantastic experience. So many good people involved."

Peggy Myers from Hillsborough was a great calming influence on the governing board, according to John. "She and her husband did some fantastic things – an amazing lady. She started **Breadbasket**, the group that would go to supermarkets in Central County to collect food that markets would otherwise throw away." That became a basic source of their meals so they didn't have to spend that much money on food.

Peggy said she started Breadbasket with two friends, **Eleanor Kauffman** and **Jane Goldberg** and they helped feed the kids at Turnbull. They went to different food markets and told the managers they were starting a food program for needy people. Knowing markets threw out an incredible amount of food they said they would be happy to pick up their leftovers. Some markets were wonderful and cooperative and some said, "Sorry, not interested; we are worried about insurance and liability," even though they were covered by the school's liability insurance. "Safeway was wonderful. Draeger's has always been wonderful by giving us a lot of food. Molly Stone co-owner **Dave Bennett** was good. I won't mention those who wouldn't support us."

John initially thought they would record everyone who came for meals, and they had a box encouraging people to contribute. They junked that effort after three months and opened the door to whoever came. John felt if someone was willing to spend their nights at a community table he didn't care what they were there for or why. At the very beginning at North Shoreview School they'd get kids because Evelyn Taylor would encourage whole families to come for a meal. Evelyn was one of those principals who knew everybody who came to her school and their backgrounds and she would get the families to come.

Walter Heyman, a long term Board member, with his wife and son initially served food on weekends and holidays at a school dining room. Walter saw that John clearly needed administrative help and told him he could do more than just ladle food. John responded that housing and feeding clients were the two areas where he needed help.

Walter thought building the food supply would be easy. All he would need to do is write letters to the CEOs of companies that are providers and distributors of food and ask them for damaged food or stuff that is beyond the date limit. He thought Samaritan House could store it and use it. So he wrote the letters, but "that didn't work at all." He didn't get any responses. He thought one CEO writing to another would get an immediate response – but he got nothing.

Walter then formed a twelve-plus person committee all connected in some way to the food industry – an owner of a confectioners shop, a restaurant owner and the folks from Village Pub in Woodside. "Then we got food by the ton. It was a fun and active committee." They put together a production kitchen and the committee members were very helpful in selecting and getting the equipment for free or at a very good price. "We wound up feeding something like five hundred persons a day then and still do today at various locations."

For many years John held a successful annual fundraiser in a giant tent in San Mateo Central Park. Almost every year **Dennis Berkowitz** from **Max's Restaurants** would bring and serve the prepared food. Both Dennis and his wife Janis were involved. They would bring a crew of over twenty paid workers along with many volunteers.

Bill Schwartz remembers a different sort of food fund raiser. He said that every year Samaritan House had a turkey drive asking folks to bring fresh or frozen turkeys for Thanksgiving distribution. They had this big outside walk-in refrigerator full of turkeys and one night somebody broke the lock and took all the turkeys. This was written up in the *San Mateo Times* and then about three times as many turkeys came into Samaritan House as were taken in the heist. So Bill told John, "Maybe we should have an annual turkey heist."

Breadbasket is still in operation after more than twenty-five years, still run by Peggy. She says a volunteer goes to Safeway, one to Piazza Market and one to Trader Joe's, who she says, "gives us a lot these days." They deliver everything to **Ruby Kaho**, the Samaritan House Kitchen Manager "who can really run a kitchen."

Now not many kids come to dinner but Samaritan House delivers meals to families and shut-ins. School locations have since become unavailable and meals are now served at the San Mateo Westside Church of Christ across from the King Center. Meals are sent twice a week to serve South San Francisco, InnVision Shelter Network's Family Place and other locations – kind of a Meals On Wheels.

Even though St. Anthony's helped early on and grocery stores participated with their "surplus" it became necessary to raise funds to support the growing population of those in need. Initial support came from the City and County and a grant from the Peninsula Community Foundation but more was needed. John started fundraising around Christmas 1985 and with volunteers sent out some three hundred letters. John began giving talks at service clubs and churches, so gradually Samaritan House began to build their support base. Volunteers came in to work at the dining room.

John said the biggest thing then needed to support the fledging Samaritan House was getting their image out to the public. John thinks they were the first or close to the first agency to distribute a newsletter, a quarterly that let people know who they were. "We just told the stories and put an envelope in there if people wanted to contribute but we didn't ask them for money." They had a P.O. Box in downtown San Mateo and the week after they sent a newsletter the mail box was jammed. John credits **Lucile Hilliard** and says, "She had ten or eleven kids; she was one of our first volunteers at our dining room. She used her expertise as a newspaper person to put our newsletter together. She was fabulous." Then the Board of Realtors would print it for them free of charge. "Those kinds of things kept happening."

The City of San Mateo first showed great support with *general* fund contributions but switched funding to *special* funds. John told **Jim Nantell,** then Assistant City Manager, that "he saw the handwriting on the wall." And by the early Nineties during a financial crunch, the City asked why they were spending all this money on Samaritan House. At that point John had to "… every bloody year go around and talk to every city councilperson to maintain our income."

Through John's efforts, and eventually the efforts of an active Board of Directors, Samaritan House fund-raising became so successful that they no longer needed government money as a primary source. "That made all the difference in the world," John says, "My philosophy on human service is if you are going to be effective: be based in the community; get the community to support what you are doing; make the community be not only the fiscal but the energy supply." They had many programs conducive to volunteerism so eventually they had "six, seven, eight hundred people a month" doing something for Samaritan House. When there was a government financial crunch John would say, "You guys may suffer but we don't have to suffer because we are paying for ourselves."

John's political philosophy is "to have government involved as little as possible – in anything. So that makes me a Republican (joke)." (*No, that makes you a Libertarian.*) John adds that the problem is that "the private sector has less interest in really doing its job. So we fall back on Democrats who are at least pretending they are setting up services. They develop bureaucracies that don't work and consume resources and so we are stuck with nothing," he says, only partly tongue in cheek.

"The unique thing about Samaritan House, and to some degree Shelter Network and HIP Housing, is that we are a private non-profit run by the community." Every single Board member has been involved in developing some part of their program. Bill Schwartz, for example, championed the clinic. They had **Louis Weil, Dennis and Janis Berkowitz**, Walter Heyman and others. They got a great many community people committed to the organization. What made the Board members and volunteers special was that they felt ownership; they were part of what Samaritan House was doing. According to John, "The amount of attention we got from people once they got connected with Samaritan House was amazing." John would go talk to groups and get them invested; that's what made Samaritan House unique as an agency. John also networked and contributed by serving on the Shelter Network Board of Directors and interacting with the Second Harvest Food Bank.

Pam Frisella says, "John sort of brought all of us into the fold. Even though he wasn't one of the founding fathers – he came in a tiny bit after – he became Mr. Samaritan House. When he came in it blossomed. He won't take any of the credit but he took it from its embryonic stage" and stayed for fifteen years.

When Samaritan House ran low on funds, long-time Board member Walter Heyman said John would pick up the phone and call "an ex-student or somebody he married or whose child he had christened. That was his way of raising funds."

There was one room in their temporary buildings at North Humboldt where they could hold Board meetings. But it was "disruptive because we had the pantry and then the kitchen there too. So we had a good number of the meetings in my office." Walter was then President of Alumax.

Samaritan House always had over two thousand volunteers, who according to Walter, often developed into donors and some into serious donors. They certainly had an alliance with the agency that was a lasting one. Even if they just handed out toys at Christmastime a real relationship developed. That was significant because "when it came to fund raising – ten dollars or a hundred dollars – they all participated."

Bill Kenney, San Mateo attorney, was another early Samaritan House Board member and served for eighteen years. Bill met Evelyn Taylor serving on the San Mateo/Foster City Elementary School District Board in the Seventies. Later, Evelyn was President of the Board of Samaritan House and asked Bill to join. Bill and John Kelly both had a Serra connection since Bill had attended high school there (before John's arrival).

Bill is a Catholic and on the National Cabinet of the Guidepost Foundation for the Norman Vincent Peale Church. Bill believes in tithing and the gospels but, like John, even more in "how we make this spirituality work in the modern world. How we help people." Bill, as the only attorney on the Board, counseled John on legal issues, always cautioning John that his advice was "worth exactly what Samaritan House paid for it – nothing."

Bill said that the Samaritan House team was doing "God's work in feeding the hungry and taking care of the poor and we had to trust in God that the money would come. I believe that God sees to it that the money comes."

Bill's other key and prescient advice was not to depend on the government for money, "So we didn't. We basically relied on the community for money." Samaritan House wrote grants for funding community counselors and for the permanent homeless shelter.

Bill said they held an annual retreat but the resulting "strategic plan really didn't make much difference because John was doing what he wanted and what he and we thought would work." John and the Board worried about their temporary kitchen and office facilities and what their landlord school district might do. That was always in the background – whether they'd get a notice to move.

Bob Fitzgerald, also a long time and active Board member, was impressed with John's optimism and confidence that, if we did good work, financial support would be there. Bob recalls in the early Nineties a number of Board meetings discussing two key issues: lack of predictable funding and John's insistence on more and expanded programs to meet the ever-growing needs. John would be asked how a new program would be paid for and he would say, don't worry, they'd get the money somewhere. "Incredibly, we were able to continue and even expand programs. His optimism was catching! We expanded a number of programs, especially the hot food distribution and medical clinic. We even started looking for a building to buy, so we could expand clinic services!"

John tells people that he could never ever have done what he did at Samaritan House if he had still been connected with the Catholic Church. "By the time you get permission to blow your nose or scratch your butt you can't get anything done." When they wanted to expand the clinic next to St. Anthony's Church in Menlo Park, "the pastor was all gung ho, the church council was all gung ho," but John had to get permission from the San Francisco Archdiocese. So John made contact and in return got a letter asking what they were doing as far as abortion and birth control and John said, "I am not bothering; I am not going to get into this; forget it – I am not going to waste my time."

Brian Cahill, who volunteers with John at San Quentin and who ran Catholic Charities in San Francisco, "went through more than his share of hell because he was trying to allow certain people *(gays)* to adopt children, and he had issues around birth control." John adds his classic line: if the Church gave up its hang-up on sex and dealt with injustice they might accomplish something.

John organized programs that fed the hungry and along the way helped many people one-on-one.

Six

Albert Odom, an Early Success

John's story would not be complete without examples of men John personally helped. As John was beginning his work at Samaritan House he met a hungry and trouble-prone little kid. John noticed and helped this youngster. You might say he saved him. Today he calls him his adopted son. This is one of three stories of redemption of which John is most proud. Most of it is unedited and in the first person voices of Albert Odom, John Kelly, and City of San Mateo Chief of Police Susan Manheimer.

Albert came to my house to be interviewed. He is a lively, alert young man. I found him friendly and eager to talk about his "adopted dad," John Kelly.

Albert Odom first met John Kelly when Albert was in the second grade. John had established the first Samaritan House kitchen at Turnbull School in San Mateo, California, and his kitchen crew would set up for meals after school was over. There was a group of mostly black neighborhood kids who would use the school grounds to play basketball. On the days meals were served the kids would come in and eat; a few would help clean up and then leave so they could play ball. John says, "These boys had a tendency to give me a bad time; they were not always cooperative.

"One of these kids, a North Shoreview School student, was a sort of protégé of the school's principal Evelyn Taylor. This kid was one of five, same mother but five different fathers. The kids all were living with their grandmother who suddenly passed away of a heart attack. These boys were then left back with their mother who was not especially attentive." So Albert would tell John stories about sleeping in motels, how his mother's boyfriend would come over and kick him out of bed so that he had to sleep on the floor. As it turned out John and Albert became real buddies. John says, "He wound up at CYA (California Youth Authority). We stayed in touch. He got out of CYA and we got back into close touch. He is now working for a plasma research company, has two sons; he's one of the best fathers I've ever met. He's one of my adopted kids." John and Albert remain bosom buddies.

Albert now lives in Hayward, California and works in San Mateo County. His oldest son is in the seventh grade and John promised Albert he would try to get his son into Serra High School. Here is Albert Odom's story and how he connected with John early in his life. It also tells a lot about John as a spiritual and caring human being:

"I'm Albert Odom and I've been around San Mateo my whole life.

I've known John most of my life – since I was in the second grade. When Samaritan House was on Delaware Street they used to have this kumquat tree. And in my back yard the fences all connected. So we used to walk down the fence and steal the kumquats. And John used to tell us to stay off the fence. Samaritan House also had an entry ramp and we used to ride our skateboards up and down that ramp. My very first experience with John was him telling us to keep the skateboards off the ramp and stay off the fence.

"But we really became close when I was in the third grade. When Samaritan House opened their first kitchen over at Turnbull, I used to break in there. I'd steal all the ice cream and steal the sandwiches in the unlocked refrigerator. John knew exactly who it was doing the stealing because we also used to go there to eat. We were breaking the law, stealing stuff and playing basketball there because we knew nobody was going to come by that late. Even though we were in the third and fourth grades, that shows what kind of parents we had to still be out at ten and eleven o'clock at night.

"To this day I believe the reason I was doing what I was doing at Turnbull was because I knew how kind-hearted this man was. I knew that he wasn't going to do anything to me. I really didn't have a relationship with him until he pulled me into that back office. There had been probably ten or twelve of us but for some reason he picked me. He says now that he knew I was their leader. I said I was the youngest of all of them but he said he could see that they were following me. So on that day John told me, 'Look, you don't have to keep breaking in here. If you want the extra ice cream and food just help (custodian) Freeman clean up after everybody leaves.' So that's what I did. I helped clean up after everybody left, mopped the floors and put the tables up. I was only in third grade. Then I was able to take the ice cream and the extra food home. Also John opened the gym for me to play basketball. I didn't know anybody who would tell a kid that we didn't have to steal.

"I expected to be punished. I knew that John knew it was us because he used to look at us and talk to us, but he never said anything. I guess he got to a point where he had to stop us from breaking in. He had an office with a back door and for some reason all we had to do was stick a card in there and it would come right open. He knew that we weren't taking anything besides food so he basically said you guys can have the leftover food – just help clean up. Earn what you get. 'Do me a favor and I'll do you a favor.' To this day when me and John talk about it we crack up. I don't know if I'd let somebody break into my job without calling the police on them. It's just not in me, but that's the kind of person John has always been.

"John already knew me and knew my grandmother because we used to go to get the bags of food at the Turnbull kitchen since we lived just around the corner. Sometimes we'd eat there with my mom and my grandmother. I really didn't know how much a part of my life he was until I got transferred to North Shoreview (School). Mrs. Taylor was close to my grandmother and she was also close to John. When I messed up in school I knew Mrs. Taylor and John were always there. And over the years John and I became very close. He has just always been there.

"After the third grade I lived with my mom which was a difficult situation for a child growing up. John doesn't talk about my mom but I'm pretty sure he doesn't really like her because she used to go up to Samaritan House, fight with the employees and act like everybody owed her something. John would say, 'What's wrong with your mom?' But he never dismissed me. John had a worker named Denise and one day she wouldn't give my mom a voucher. So my mom started fighting with this woman inside Samaritan House. John never held it against me for what my mom did there and she did a lot.

"I got into a lot of trouble in first, second and third grade at Laurel School. I used to throw chairs and one time I jumped up on the roof. John was at Laurel that day and they called John and my uncle and everybody to get me down off the roof. I was just sitting there taunting the teachers. I was a very angry kid. That's maybe the reason I was able to straighten my life up so soon. I did so much when I was a kid.

"John was always there for me. When I was in third grade I got kicked out of Laurel School. There was a man who worked for John, and John had him mentoring me; he would come up to the school and get me. When I got kicked out, John and Evelyn Taylor thought it would be best for me to go to North Shoreview School where they could watch over me. John was close to Mrs. Taylor who was the principal and John was always at North Shoreview. Actually I started doing very good in school and then my grandmother died when I was in the fourth grade. Then my life went topsy-turvy. John and I agree that from that point I was just an angry kid. I became a real problem and not just for my mom. She was doing her best to try to take care of me and my brothers. But at the same time she was on drugs and drugs run your life.

"I moved away to Los Angeles for a while. I lived for two years with my dad who had come home from prison. Then he went back to prison and I came back here and I was a floater because my mom did not have a place to stay and I was living with her in different places. John always made sure my mom had vouchers to stay at a room over at the (then) Royal Lodge (motel). Because of the life I was in I ended up selling drugs, and even though I was doing good in middle school I was still getting into a lot of trouble. Through those middle school years John was there but when I started selling drugs we lost contact for a while. I spent almost a year at Hillcrest Juvenile Hall and went to trial while they sorted out the true from the not-true charges. So I ended up in CYA (California Youth Authority – jail for juveniles) when I was fifteen.

"After about four months in CYA in Stockton I got a letter from John saying he had been trying to find out where I was. He really took care of me when I was in CYA. I didn't really have anybody, nobody writing me except for friends who write you only for so long. John started coming to visit me and writing to me. It felt good. I felt wanted. I always tell John that with him I always felt wanted. I always felt appreciated. He was never just some passerby who would help you and then move on.

"It was funny when I was due to get out. I was supposed to be in there for two years, but I got in trouble and got an extra six months. But then after that extra six months when I was supposed to get out nobody in my family would let me stay with them, so I didn't have an address. So I stayed yet another six months. I was calling everybody and they were saying they didn't want that trouble. And I was a troublesome kid.

"Of course I could have lived with my dad in Los Angeles, but that was a totally different life style and my dad was a gang banger. I didn't like Los Angeles at all. Especially being the kind of person I had become. The stuff I was doing here could have been enhanced and made worse in Los Angeles.

"I wound up talking to one of my cousins, **LaRonn**, and he got with John and they both agreed we could make this work. So I was able to get out of jail in January of 1996 with the help of John and my cousin. By the time I came home to San Mateo John had a job for me that I started about two weeks after I got out: my very first job ever, at Wisnom's (now Ace) Hardware Store. John knew co-owner **Dick Nelson** who offered me a job and I was there for a year and a half. I sat down with Dick Nelson, John told him the whole situation, and even Dick Nelson took a chance on me. It worked out good: I picked up skills and a trade. I learned how to build barbeques. Dick helped me get my first driver's license. So John put me in a great situation.

"It was strange at first. I had never had to be at a certain place at a certain time. When I first started there I was always late back from lunch. No matter what, I was always late from my hour lunch break. For some reason I would always go all the way home for lunch. It was a learning process. Dick used to call me in his office and say you can't do this, you can't do that, but he never fired me or let me go. He just always explained, 'Look as long as you're working here you've got to do this and got to do that.' In a year and a half I learned a lot. It was great. I've only had two jobs in my life and Wisnom's was the first. Later I'd still go in and talk to Dick and **Suzi Nelson** and everybody else there.

"In 1997 I got off a BART train. I was still on CYA parole. I had seen a guy who I was in CYA with and I stopped and talked to him. He walked away, the police rushed him and the cop who had him on the ground said, 'Get him too, get him too,' meaning me. I had nothin' to do with nothin'. And I went back to jail. I had to go before the Parole Board in front of **Panetta** – the guy who works for Obama. I got a violation because I had come in contact with police. Even though the police didn't bring charges against me or anything, I still went back to CYA because I got in contact with them. I was there for three months and Dick Nelson still kept my job for me. Dick and John believed that I really hadn't done anything. I just stopped and talked to this guy; I didn't know he was selling drugs.

"John had come to my Parole Board meeting with me. I remember going in front of Panetta and him asking me, 'Did you do it?' When you go in front of the Parole Board they want you to say yes, whether you did it or not. They want you to admit to it. But I told him no, I didn't do anything. He had me leave the room. I don't know what happened between Panetta and John but I think he asked John, 'Would you trust him inside your house?' And John told him yes. I remember walking back into the Board meeting and I thought that I wasn't going to get out because I didn't admit to it. He grilled me: 'Why don't you want to admit to it?' But I got paroled. John was sitting to my left and my wife next to him and **Nancy Rosenbledt** who was my counselor at Borel Middle School who has been a part of my life since then. Panetta put his pen down and says, 'I believe you. And the reason I believe you is because this gentleman (John) says he would trust you inside his house. And I trust him.' I'd gone in December 2, 1997 and I got out February 18, 1998 and I've never been back since. When Panetta said I was going to be released 'today' I remember running back to get my stuff and all of us walking out to the parking lot. I was so thankful for the conversation that went on between him and John.

"When I was back in CYA I was back to being angry. I felt I had been violated because I hadn't done anything. They had me sitting there for so long. My birthday was December fourteenth. I went through my birthday; I went through Christmas; I went through my wife's birthday. I was held at (CYA) NRCC in Sacramento. And John came all the way to Sacramento to help me out.

"That was all in the past, but when John tried to get me cleared to go with him into San Quentin, even though my record had been expunged since I was a juvenile, because it was drugs my record still comes up with the government. They sent John a notice that I could not come in because I'm a known drug trafficker. This was 2009, 2010, and my offense was 1994. That shows that a person like John forgives but our society never moves on. 'If he did it then there is a chance he'll do it again.' I got stopped for a traffic stop and one of the first things the cop asked me was did I have any drugs in the car. I said no, why? He said it comes up that you are a known drug trafficker. I asked if it said when that happened. He said no it just comes up that you are a known drug trafficker. I said I was fourteen and that was 1994. I don't let it get to me because I have no intention of getting stopped for traffic. I always look at it that I should have stopped at that stop sign.

"By then I had matured a lot and had started a family. I got married at age nineteen and have stayed married now for fifteen years. I have two sons, one thirteen years old and one eighteen months, and they call John 'grand paw.' John has been with me and my wife ever since. From Wisnom's I started a job at 4th State in Belmont doing plasma research. I started that job in 1999 and that's where I'm still at.

"My oldest son is getting A's and B's and John is trying to get him into Serra High School. He and John talk about that constantly. John is after him to learn Spanish. John often comes over for dinner, and my wife enjoys the fact that he is very comfortable. John helped us get our first place. When we first started neither of us had credit. So John let us use his credit for our first car and for my first motorcycle and for our first apartment. He's really been a part of my life and now also my wife's and kids'.

"John and I get together for lunch usually every other Friday. I'm meeting him at noon at Fresh Choice. He hates his walker and if I wait for him he says, 'What are you waiting for.' And I have to back off. He likes being independent. My family dies early. My grandma died at fifty and my mom died at forty-eight. I appreciate the fact that John wants to do stuff for himself. 'If the body can move then I can do it. If I need your help then I'll let you know.'

"Our family is not very health conscious. My Auntie has high blood pressure and diabetes and all this stuff. But every week we have a fish fry and we have a BBQ where there are ribs and sweet potato pies. I was overweight and I couldn't play basketball with my son and thought, I don't want to be like this, knowing throughout my life my whole family had been like this. I'm thirty-five and now every morning me and my wife get up at 4:45 and go to 24 Hour Fitness and work out. My son plays basketball and I coach Terra Linda and also coach Team Esface and coach the Bayside Broncos football team. So it is coaching and running and just staying active. We started running the football team up at Edgewood Park and I had to impress them, so that's when I started running. A lot of it had to do with setting an example for my eighth grade son. He's slimmed down and he's at the gym right now.

"I worry about John because he is so forgiving. I believe that some people are getting out of jail, going back, getting out and going back. I always tell

John there is a point where you've got to say that this guy isn't going to make it. John says you can't look at it like that. I say that I can because I was part of that same system. John always tells me that I'm different. But I don't feel different. I don't like people closing doors behind me, telling me what to do, telling me how to live. And I don't care for hurting other people. We talk about a lot of the other people John deals with and I wonder how he deals with people who are in and out (of prison), in and out and John is always right there for them. I don't know if it is a jealousy thing for me or that I just want John to be careful. I tell John that if he had stayed a priest he could have been a saint. I don't know even a priest that has the kind of heart that he has. He has a very big heart.

"John is very selfless. It is never, 'I'm doing this because of this or that.' He thinks everybody has good in him. For some people it doesn't come out or comes out in different ways. John sees good in people and says, 'If you want good to come out, stick with me.' And being around John, it is very easy to do good. Like me, I live to impress him. I like the fact that he comes over to my house and plays with my kids. We actually joke that at all the birthday parties the other guests comment that John is the only white guy there. 'Who is that, the school principal?' John just sits there and cracks up and plays with the kids.

"It is funny when we are out to lunch, and we're sitting there cracking up and talking about this and that. We'll look around and laugh at the people looking at us wondering what we have in common with each other. I don't know exactly what it is with John. I just know that he is a very selfless person. His whole goal in life is that the world can be a better place."

John adds that when Albert came back to San Mateo, he became very active in the old North Central neighborhood "as in wanting to change it. Albert was particularly taking on the police department who he thought were racist as hell and profiling like crazy. He would come to public meetings and he incurred the displeasure of a certain chief of police as a result." It reached a point where John was told by the chief of police that John was ruining his reputation by associating with him. Albert finally moved to San Carlos from North Central and then to Hayward, because he didn't want his kids raised in that earlier environment.

San Mateo Chief of Police, Susan Manheimer, remembers Albert and his transition, and here's her point of view:

I asked her for a story about when she and John Kelly got crosswise: "I will not mention the name of the individual. John will laugh – he will know this story. And I think about this one often. I am conflicted myself about this one because I believe in redemption, and if I didn't policing would be a very tough profession. If the truth be known, most cops are fairly optimistic because if they weren't they just couldn't do this job anymore. So I tell them if it starts to get brutal, get out because it's miserable. So we all really truly believe in lots of ways of helping. So when you have someone you have to give up on, or say enact the consequences for, it can be tough because there is not always a right answer. Because the people themselves need to change and for some reason they don't.

"There was one young man whom John mentored through a childhood of likely violence, certainly felony behavior, in our own North Central neighborhood, terrorizing and influencing other youth in a negative way, being loud mouthed and a troublemaker. He spent time in and out of prison and I'm guessing that's where John first got to know him through his work with prisoners and re-entry. And so this young man came back out a changed individual. He was brought here to speak at Rotary and was actually a compelling and inspirational speaker. John got him into the Leadership San Mateo Program and some other incredible things, really giving him the chance that he'd never had.

"All laudable, right? In Leadership Program he started getting a bit more critical of issues. We had some concerns that he was still involved in some of those earlier activities. I talked to John about that. I did not feel that it was appropriate to bring him back into the civic culture without him committing to a social contract to no longer misbehave and no longer influence the young kids out there. They were all looking at him as a role model. So John and I had a big disagreement about that. And I think he thought I was being a hard-assed cop which I was. And I thought he was being the weak liberal which he was. And sometimes there is just going to be that divide. But I think at the end of the day, and I hope John feels the way I do, I respected where his position was and I understood…. It's almost like a prosecution and defense. You must have both for the justice system and checks and balances to work. And I think that's where John and I are and I totally respect and am delighted that he would advocate for these individuals. Somebody needs to do it."

I have a hunch you are talking about Albert Odom? "I couldn't mention any names. I hope he is doing very well. All power to him. As I said, I believe in redemption. I also believe that you have to enact some social contracts and consequences. If you want to be in influential circles, if you want to be someone at a level of impact and influence, there is responsibility that goes with that."

Were there times at a community meeting or other social situations where he was not appropriate? "I don't remember all the details. I think there were some disappointing moments when he seemed to be very much upset and angry over whatever it was. And I don't know that he was able to channel that appropriately. But in finding your voice and working within what is really a close knit community there are certainly opportunities for opposition and divergent points of view. God bless us; we would be lost without that. We'd be a repressive regime.

"I told John that if Albert wants to be part of this community he should make that step and then work within it. He had a misstep with **Mayor John Lee**; he started attacking some issue or program. I think it had to do with the police and the Mayor took issue with it but Albert kept going at it for about ten minutes. It was unfortunate but again I do believe in redemption. I have nothing but the best hope for Albert. And I hope he is doing well because I think he is a very inspiring and influential young man in our North Central. All I say is: Use your influence for good. We've often talked about wanting to do more especially within our African-American community looking for those who would do outreach and work with our youth. I think there are still, at times, tensions between the communities and the police. It would be nice if Albert would commit to be one of those facilitators and bridges who would outreach to this community. We have been successful in many of our diverse communities in San Mateo using those individuals as bridges.

"I could see that Albert was starting out his second life, a new entry into public life in a way he could influence people. And I thought it really important that he not blow that opportunity and just go back with some negative habits. And that was when I first talked to John about it. I didn't want to see this young man misinformed about the way he could really help. I had heard this young man be so inspiring here at our Rotary he got a standing ovation. And then to see that tape of the community meeting with the Mayor, it was so disappointing. This is not going to help him. It's not going to help us. It won't be a bridge. So that was when I said to John: Think about this. Is this really good for him or for the community? That was really my intent. It was never to say don't hold out a hand and don't allow for redemption."

Albert Odom was among the first of the hungry people John fed through Samaritan House. But John could see that the poor in San Mateo County needed clothes as well as food.

Seven

Clothing the Naked, Housing the Homeless, Healing the Sick

Samaritan House formed a clothes closet for parents and children first in a gym, then a twice yearly "Super Saturday" warehouse distribution, then to a purple house (Purple Palace) shared with Shelter Network. That was followed for a number of years by a rented building on Norfolk Avenue just across the street from North Shoreview School. **Lucille Francard** started volunteering for Samaritan House when she was about eighty years old and she became the boss of that clothes closet. Department stores would be envious at how she had that thing set up and how she managed the crew of about five other lady workers. John remembers the day of the 1989 earthquake when he went there and roof timbers had fallen in, narrowly missing Lucille, and the place was a disaster.

The Clothes Closet, in 1994-5, moved to a retail/warehouse building on South Claremont Street, San Mateo. The City approved a zoning or use change but required a community meeting to let people know what was happening. Before John went to the meeting at nearby Sunnybrae School he went and sat by the bay and prayed, "Lord make sure you keep me safe." Two to three hundred people showed up, mostly young families. As John walked in there was this gentleman standing by the door. He gave a polite hello but looked at John with a scowl and said, "If the original owner of this building knew what you were doing he would turn over in his grave."

The meeting began with people screaming at John and his team for ruining and destroying the neighborhood. A lady who lived farther north on Claremont Street was what John called "one of the three witches of Endor." Her story was, "Well, I've already seen two homeless people sitting in their car just waiting for the Closet to open and they are going to be coming like crazy." All kinds of rules and regulations were required about how the place was run in order to keep the neighbors happy. When the homeless winter shelter was open, Samaritan House had a rule that no single persons could go down to the clothes closet building on their own. So Friday was singles day. A community worker would drive the homeless persons there, wait until they got their clothes and then drive them back again. John says, "Afterward, we never ever had an official complaint from a neighbor about how we ran that building."

About that time a lady in her late nineties with a fair amount of money from running rest homes told her lawyer she had no relatives except a niece who never paid her any attention. "So find me some charities that I can give my money to." The lawyer's wife happened to have dinner with a friend of John's who suggested Samaritan House be added to the lawyer's list of suggested charities. Soon afterward the woman died and left them about ten percent of her estate, a few hundred thousand dollars, which was enough to buy the building." That building has since closed and Samaritan House now operates the Kids' Closet in their main building on Forty-Second Street and Pacific Boulevard in San Mateo.

Housing the Homeless

Samaritan House provided housing rental assistance for a short period of time and they used the California National Guard Armory across the street in San Mateo as a homeless shelter. After their nightly use they had to clear out all the bunks so the Army could use it during the day. The shelter residents did not have to be clean of drugs but they had to be willing to participate in drug and alcohol cessation programs. They could stay for as long as six weeks.

Sue Lempert was a San Mateo City Council member when Samaritan House ran the homeless shelter in the San Mateo Armory. The shelter created a very contentious situation for the people in the North Central neighborhood where the Armory was located. They complained about people hanging out, being dirty and responsible for crime "but many of their concerns were unfounded." Sue says that the City had always helped fund Samaritan House at thirty or thirty-five thousand dollars; in fact, some of their responsibilities were once given to in-house City staff so Samaritan House could do a better job. But during leaner years there were "three votes to cut the funding to ten or fifteen thousand dollars. But Councilmember **Janet Epstein** and I were strong Samaritan House defenders and later we restored the funding."

State Senator Jerry Hill, as a San Mateo City Councilman and then as a San Mateo County Supervisor, had substantial involvement with the homeless shelter issue. He said, "It has been over twenty-three years since I first met John Kelly. I have learned much from him. We met in the Rotary Club of San Mateo, but my education began when I became a San Mateo City Councilmember." Jerry was concerned about the use of that Armory in San Mateo as a winter homeless shelter operated by Samaritan House under contract by San Mateo County.

Jerry thought the operation of the homeless shelter presented many problems for the neighborhood and that it should be closed or moved. The Armory was limited to ninety individuals per night but sometimes a hundred and twenty would line up outside. The doors didn't open until five o'clock p.m. Those who didn't make the cut were turned away to wander the neighborhood all night "presenting problems for the residents." The next morning at around seven o'clock the ninety individuals had to leave the shelter but they didn't want to go far because they had to be in line early to be included in the ninety for the next night. Many would roam the neighborhood, camp out at the nearby Martin Luther King Center or hide away out of sight.

Jerry voiced his concerns to John on numerous occasions and in John's priestly manner he would invite Jerry into his world to spend some time and see how people struggle to get by. John explained how dealing with the various challenges had brought them to the point of homelessness. Whether it was substance abuse, unemployment, mental or medical illness, there is very little support or help available on a long-term basis to allow these struggling individuals to turn their lives around. The Armory was the best available site that offered some shelter from the nighttime winter weather.

Jerry said, "I gained an understanding of the homeless problem, but I also wanted to resolve some of the neighborhood issues. The area around the Armory was teeming with homeless people and the neighbors wanted some relief."

Jerry worked with John, then **San Mateo County Supervisor Ted Lempert** and county staff to develop operational controls for the use of the Armory as a winter shelter. They initiated a program for St. Vincent de Paul to distribute ninety shelter vouchers each day. This eliminated the need for people to come to the Armory to stand in line.

With encouragement from Jerry, help was also provided by SamTrans. Each morning when the homeless individuals left the Armory, SamTrans provided bus passes so they could leave the area for work or other reasons. This relieved the congestion in the vicinity and resolved many of the neighborhood concerns.

A few years later as a San Mateo County Supervisor, Jerry had the responsibility of the human services needs of San Mateo County. With those new responsibilities, he undertook the difficult task of finding a site to build and operate a year-round county homeless shelter.

Jerry said, "Working with John, then **South San Francisco Mayor Gene Mullin**, and SamTrans, we located a site in South San Francisco at the SamTrans bus maintenance facility near the airport." Jerry then helped cobble together the necessary funding and, "to this day, we have a ninety-bed, year-round homeless shelter in San Mateo County which is largely self-sustaining."

Healing the Sick

Samaritan House community workers became aware of clients, particularly the undocumented, who were not getting good medical attention.

Doctors Bill Schwartz and **Walter Gaines** (R.I.P.) were both attached to Mills Hospital and with their help in 1989 John developed a committee to see about starting their own clinic.

Bill Kenney says that starting a medical clinic was a big venture for Samaritan House and they had to trust that this was what Samaritan House was supposed to be doing. "Let's take a chance on it and see what it is like. And so that's what we did. And John was always willing to go along because he too felt the Divine Providence the way I do. When you think of Samaritan House and where it started, where it was and where it is now, it has been a really amazing transition. The medical clinic was a big step forward."

Bill Schwartz was an MD with a former private practice in San Mateo, an early Samaritan House Board Member and spark plug for the first medical clinic. Bill saw an article by John in the San Mateo County Medical Bulletin reporting that Samaritan House really needed a clinic. In private practice from 1961 to 1993 Bill always felt badly that he could not take care of more indigent and needy patients. Bill got in touch with John, found mutual interest and they worked together for about four years to get the clinic off the ground.

Bill said the first problem was finding a place and they thought they might find something with the **San Mateo County (Chope) Hospital** – if they could work with them. "But they were worse than not helpful because they would say yes that is a good idea and we will do that. But when it came to the reality they weren't there: 'Oh no, we can't do that.'" Bill asked to coordinate medical records with the hospital and asked for a copy of their blank chart. The answer was: "Oh no, we have to get permission from the hospital board of directors." Bill said they would tell you up front they would do it and then they wouldn't do it.

Bill practiced at **Mills Peninsula** and **UCSF** Hospitals and thought it strange that it took "two or three years before they would license me at the County Medical Center." Bill always thought that the clinic would be a wonderful idea. But the big lesson he learned and passed on to John was that the County was really not interested in having any competition, especially competition that they didn't understand. That is, a free clinic to take care of needy people. *(John Kelly thinks that government regulations kept the hospital from responding as Samaritan House would have liked.)*

Bill thinks the hospital didn't fully understand and thought the clinic might take away their patients and their jobs. The County would always demand to be paid – to charge their regular fees. John and his committee nearly said, "Let's just forget it." Bill said, "There were doctors on their Board and I didn't really get to talk to them but it seemed that they really didn't want to do it and they were going to block it but they didn't want us to think that." Bill said from that point forward he thought that if you are going to start a project, "leave government out of it. Do as much as possible with the private sector." Now, Bill reports cordial relations with the County hospital and says they send patients in for surgery and "it now works out OK."

John was a goal oriented person with "tremendous leadership skills and a good partner in the clinic project." He'd say to Bill, "That's where we want to go. I can't follow all those things. You and whoever you work with are going to have to get us there." And they would get there because John wanted them to get there. Much went without words. At the Samaritan Board meetings, Bill said that John would be there and on his side with a "mostly supportive" Board.

Bill said he moved the County hospital folks aside and talked to others to get support and find a place for the clinic. Liability insurance for a clinic at a cost of $25,000 was initially a big issue. Bill talked to **Al Horn** (of Carr, McClellan, Ingersoll, Thompson & Horn) about the insurance and Al said he might be able to get them covered under the Mills Hospital policy. Bill explained what Samaritan House wanted to do and Mills took them under their umbrella and recruited Mills doctors and nurses to work at their clinic for free. Those doctors and nurses were covered under the Mills Hospital insurance policy.

Bill talked to **Bob Merwin, CEO** of Mills-Peninsula Hospitals (Mills and Peninsula Hospitals merged in 1985) and said SmithKline Beecham Clinical Laboratories was doing the clinic lab work but just for a short time. Bob said Peninsula Hospital should be doing that lab work. So Peninsula took over and they continue to provide the clinic with laboratory and x-ray services. Bill says those services are key and that you can't practice modern medicine without them. "Bob has been extremely helpful all along the way." When the hospital got new equipment and furniture Bob gave the excess to the clinic. Bill said they have had "a very amicable relationship with Mills-Peninsula Hospitals."

In 1992 they got the clinic off the ground using a room in one of the temporary portables on Humboldt Street. During the day the room was used for meals and all sorts of uses. In the evening they pushed aside the tables, brought in other tables and put in partitions and curtains. The Humboldt Street Clinic started with one evening a week, then, according to John Kelly, added a couple more nights and continued there for about five years before deciding they needed their own separate clinic. Doctor Walter Gaines took on the task of getting a new clinic declared official, even finding the clinic's own insurance policy and expanding the number of doctors who could work there. John said, "The paperwork amounted to the founding of a brand new hospital." They rented an office space on North San Mateo Drive and started their own official facility. **Sheryl Young**, now CEO of **Community Gatepath**, had connections with Mills-Peninsula Hospital and helped get them into this office space at a reduced price. John said he was not sure they were paying any rent. That clinic really flourished.

Bill says, "We take care of many patients early in the course of their illness so they don't get sicker and end up in the emergency room with its $10,000 bill." They are actually able to reduce costs by taking care of patients early. They also treat people with communicable diseases which might spread into the community if the clinic was not there.

Bill once spoke at a League of Women Voters event and an audience member asked, "Are you encouraging all these people to come across the border to your clinic?" Bill said he was upset about and didn't agree with what was happening at the border. But he added that when people are in the community and they are sending their children to school and they are ill, "as doctors we have a responsibility to take care of people. We don't ask questions because we are a local community and we are not speaking for the State or the Nation." He added that when people are in your community, they are part of your community, and the clinic doesn't ask whether or not they are legal. He said he was not in favor of a 'sanctuary clinic' but if sick people came to their clinic they had to take care of them.

The clinic started recruiting specialists so they could deal with all kinds of illnesses as well as general medicine. John reports that Bob Merwin had said that Samaritan House clients were getting the best care on the Peninsula. Eye care was added and **Gerry Bundy** of Bundy Opticians offered to provide glasses at his cost. The clinic also started providing dentistry and according to John, "that is really unique in the world."

Samaritan House ultimately purchased and moved the clinic to 19 West Thirty-Ninth Avenue in San Mateo. "Buying and funding that building in 2000/2001 was one of my last acts as director. I hung around to raise the money to pay for the building." John says that the **Peninsula Health Care District** gave a fair amount of money to help pay for it.

The Director of **Sequoia Health Care District** came to John and wanted to create a similar clinic. They found a suitable building at 114 Fifth Avenue, Redwood City and Sequoia pretty much covered the whole expense. Bill Schwartz said that was a much easier proposition, "because we had the Sequoia Health Care District behind us one hundred percent. They were lovely people to work with and we had excellent help and got it started in relatively short order."

The clinic medical staff volunteers were committed, generous and shared many hours of their time. Bill Schwartz recruited doctors who were retiring and said the doctors felt "rejuvenated because they could do real medicine." They had no paperwork to worry about, and they could spend as much time as they wanted with a client. "I had more doctors tell me that the greatest thing that ever happened to them was to volunteer at Samaritan House." A great spirit was generated in the clinic and John tells people that "the psychological healing that went on there was as important as the physical healing. Can you imagine the good feelings of these people who had no other possibility of real medical care?"

Bill cherishes the thought that when John Kelly had days with especially heavy responsibilities he would get in his car and come to the San Mateo clinic. He'd see people being taken care of and that would completely change his mood and uplift him by seeing what was going on in the clinics. He did it quite often. He'd just be looking around but "he was feeling joy about what was going on. He was soaking up the good will." John called it "getting refurbished – rehabbed. Even today if you walk into that building on Thirty-Ninth Avenue, you just feel it, just walking in the door; the spirit there is fabulous. And Bill Schwartz had a lot to do with getting it all set up and generating that spirit."

On December 5, 1999 the Sunday *New York Times* wrote a two page article about Samaritan House and the clinics on the front and second pages with pictures. They sent a reporter who stayed for two days in the clinic. Articles have also been published in *Modern Maturity* and *Parade Magazine*. The clinics have also been featured on ABC's Evening News with Peter Jennings, PBS's California Connected, and CNN's Democracy in America.

John Kelly has high praise for Bill Schwartz and says: "The clinic was a perfect example of community service. If there is a need in the community and nobody else is filling it or not doing it well our Board would say, do we or don't we? Well, somebody has to do it so what the heck." Bill Kenney again reminded the Board that if the clinic is needed the community will support it. "So don't worry about the cost, we will get the money. And so the money did come from all over the place."

John Kelly Moves On
John built the fledgling effort called Samaritan House into a major independent non-profit that now operates a ninety-bed homeless shelter, two free medical clinics and a free kids' clothes closet, as well as feeding 145,000 meals a year to the hungry. An amazing 2,000 volunteers help provide these services to some 12,000 folks in need in San Mateo County. Most of the funding continues to come from private donations which insulates the

operation from the vagaries of government funding. John was ahead of the curve of government budget cutbacks and set the stage for a fiscally solvent and sustainable organization. "It helps the local community take ownership of the operation," says Kelly. He sees it as a model of neighbor helping neighbor.

At age seventy-one in 1999, after nearly fifteen years at the helm, John found himself once again in the bustle of Christmas crunch time. He said he felt tired and didn't think he could do one more holiday season. John decided it was time for him to move on, time for somebody to take over. Samaritan House had grown in complexity and now required some of the administration that John chafed against in the Catholic Church. **Kitty Lopez,** the current Executive Director of Samaritan House thinks that at some point the bureaucracy of Samaritan House had become too much for John. "I think he felt restrained by the organization."

Kitty says she learned from John, and also how she could make adaptations for today. John was very good at bringing people together including the volunteers and getting the community involved. Samaritan House in Kitty's mind has always had two missions: one is to *help* people in need and the other is to *create a community* that helps people in need. That is, "we all do this together. That's what John believes and what I believe."

Walter Heyman says that John was never an administrative whiz. John was always in charge and got important things done but his desk and office were chaotic. Walter reports that you could not see the top of John's desk which was "covered with a good eighteen inches or more of letters and manuals and paperwork." John hated administration and it showed. When John retired it took him three weeks to clean his desk. It wasn't as if he was looking for something and couldn't find it; he knew where everything was. But no one else knew where anything was.

John was justly proud of the fact that he ran the organization with an almost skeleton staff to keep overhead low. John was primarily concerned with getting maximum benefit to the poor even if administration suffered. John was laser focused on helping people in need who he thought could change their lives.

Kitty says that when Samaritan House took over running the homeless shelter they took people that most people did not want to take. John said they should take anyone who showed up. But Kitty looked at it through the lenses of the organization to make sure everybody is safe; the human resources part, the legal part. She said, "John didn't worry about all that." Kitty says that how they accommodate people right out of jail or on probation with eighty-nine other people and staff and keep everybody safe is an ongoing issue. Kitty and staff worked with John on that and "he slowly has recognized that we have this operation that we try to keep safe." The County is still working on how to bring people out of jail and integrate them back into society. Kitty says, "I don't know all the answers and I know John is intimately involved with those issues."

Kitty knows that John holds dear the idea that people can change and that their lives can be different but sometimes he doesn't care about the rest – "Oh, we'll figure it out." When Kitty took over as the third Executive Director she said there were some "employees involved in drugs who had to leave." But John was always "trying to give everybody a break. It didn't matter if they had credentials or were qualified or had the skills," John asked her, "Can you get them a job?" Kitty would ask, could they do A, B and C? John would respond, "No, but they need a job – give them a chance." And Kitty would say, "But John, we can't have these people working for the agency." But she says "that's John's role; that's his voice. And that's fine if he has that voice around the table, but if we are going to come up with a solution there have to be many voices."

Kitty said their driver got caught with drugs in the car. She documented and followed HR procedures, met with other volunteers and asked, how do I do this legally, protect the agency and do right by the employee? She wanted to document properly *and* provide chances for the person to improve. Finally she had to let him go. John had heard about it and came to the office and talked to Kitty. John had helped this guy for many years but Kitty said, "I can't have him working and using drugs and having drugs in the car. What if something happens? What about the organization?"

Kitty met with John when she first began eleven years ago because he had a big strong voice and presence in the community. She said that John left her big shoes to fill but "I didn't go down that road. John could be along beside me as I needed him to help me." They had a similar view about people and about the community and she said that John's message was always clear that "we are here to help each other. If you have extra stuff and your neighbor needed it, you gave it to him. If you needed a place to stay and I had a couch – come on over." Kitty said, "That's how John operates and how he takes that simple message about helping people, especially in their time of need. And John built that in the community."

After John retired he would still come into the kitchen and tell kitchen manager Ruby to do things and Kitty would ask him, "Can you check with me? Just check with me." John would come back and use clerical services and Kitty let it go because "he had a presence there and I welcome that. We include John in our holiday program in the community. We have an annual volunteer recognition and we always invite him."

Kitty thinks that John's voice is an important voice. "Maybe as you get older you realize that all these voices are important; that you don't have to be right or change any of them. It is important to listen and there is value in that. You wonder, if we didn't have that voice, would we think differently."

Pam Frisella says John had the stamina to have lasted more years at Samaritan House but "wasn't so computer savvy." He realized it was time and volunteered to go but he knew that he had more to give. The Board decided after John retired that they had to remove him from the spotlight. Because when John walks into a room – "he *is* Samaritan House." The reason Samaritan House is known as it is, is because of John's philosophy of not taking government dollars; of going to private foundations; for walking the walk; for showing people what it is like out there; for proving to people; for bringing in volunteers.

The Board of Directors back then each had a specific area: Pam's was always the homeless shelter; Bill Schwartz had the clinics; somebody else had the clothes closet or the kitchen. They were doing the work; they were the volunteers. Pam says, "We had the passion because we saw people not eating; we were out in the community. I didn't write big checks but I was out there." So it was more volunteer driven then and now it is more business driven. "It drives John nuts because there are so many employees now." John said he ran that place with four people. But it is much bigger now and it's very well run. Pam thinks Kitty Lopez has done "an absolute fantastic job."

To give Kitty a chance to become the new face of Samaritan House the Board kind of moved John back behind the door. Pam says, "That's all great, but they need the people involved who brought it to where it is today. They invited John to their main event last year and the place was sold out – because of John Kelly; because of the main contributors and John Kelly fans." Plus John tried to bring in the Serra High School connection so those Serra kids can see "what's really happening in the world – not in the life that they live at Serra High School."

Looking back, John claims that organizing and running Samaritan House was one more chapter that he got involved in that he did not do strictly by choice. "My arm was twisted to run the dining room, the County twisted my arm to take over the Samaritan referral service." But John adds: "I'll accept two claims to fame. One was somehow having the facility and good fortune to pick out the right people to work with Samaritan House." John says, they really knew what they were doing and had this dedication. The Board of Directors drove him nuts every once and a while, but of all the Boards he's been on he said, "God, were we blessed. We had some of the most fantastic people on our Board."

John says his second claim to fame was his being willing to work hard to spread the Samaritan House message. He was willing to go to those "dog fights" to let people know what they were doing. Most people aren't willing to work as hard as John worked. John notes that some of these human service folks "got in at 8:30 and went home at 5:00 and forgot about it." John never had a spare day in his life. There was "some value in my not having a family of my own. I could never have done that if I had a wife and kids at home."

John is justly proud of his contribution to Samaritan House and of the many Samaritan House contributions to feed, shelter and care for the health of its poorest residents.

Eight

Education and Service to Youth

John began his service to youth at Serra High School, while at Samaritan House and then continued that youth service after he left. Walter Heyman says that John was always big on education, along with Evelyn Taylor. They always had some Samaritan House activity in education. For a while they had this streaming exercise, taking kids from elementary school and making sure they were on track to get to college. The kids would spend many hours outside of school for additional education. Walter said that they made sure that the parents were involved with their kids.

Kitty Lopez says that John has always worked a lot with youth and now works with PAL (San Mateo Police Activities League) helping to tutor them as well as helping them on the soccer field. He knows that you have to do things differently with young people so they don't wind up in prison. He knows that and gets that. "I think it's the teacher in him." He is trying to do some positive things that society would agree with. John truly believes that "everyone deserves a chance no matter where they are on that continuum."

After he left his leadership role at Samaritan House John continued to be involved with education and particularly with inspiring underserved and minority kids. One example is John's work at Bayside Middle School.

Dick Nelson, former co-owner of Wisnom's Hardware, has worked alongside John Kelly at Bayside Middle School and its STEM (Science, Technology, Engineering and Mathematics) Academy in east San Mateo. This school has been adopted by the San Mateo Rotary of which both John and Dick are members. Both Rotarians tutor and mentor Bayside students. Dick says that the students of Bayside respect John because they know he means it when he makes them say in unison, "I am going to college." John is very serious about how they study. He is proud of his earlier teaching Latin and helps the students with their paper writing. Dick says John has a nice but firm way of telling a student who is playing around to get back to work. He finds student tutors and keeps them returning and setting a good example for their personal students. John reminds both tutors and students to do a good job because a Rotary scholarship could be in their future. No promise, but it puts meaning in his voice.

Dick says that after John's stroke he came to school and told the students what happened to him and how he is getting better. John is more than just a teacher; he has a style that gets students' respect as "a mentor and genuine human being."

John asks why we have so little counseling in a school where we know very well these kids have "a horrible life going on at home." They are trying to teach them Science, Technology, Engineering and Mathematics and yet not all students even get breakfast, lunch and dinner. "It's all wacky." John says that our elementary schools should have major counseling departments. "For every kid who walks into one of our east-side-of-town schools, we should know exactly what their family situation is. What are their challenges? Why are they having all these problems?" There are stories in the *San Mateo Daily Journal* about some of these kids who are going to college and some of what they had to go through to survive. John asks, "Who is paying attention to them?"

John recently interviewed every eighth grader at Bayside Middle School who is in the San Mateo Rotary SMART program. In this San Mateo Academic Rotary Team program, older students who have received the SMART award tutor younger students. The purpose of this program is to encourage promising San Mateo eighth graders, otherwise unlikely to be college bound, to prepare for college while in San Mateo high schools and then enroll in a two year or four year college.

Those kids appreciate the fact that John was willing to sit down with them one-on-one. He took the time to find out about their family life and how they were going to survive high school. Last year there were two kids in particular that **Jeanne Elliott**, Principal of Bayside Middle School and STEM Academy, asked John to meet with once a week as a sort of mini counseling. John says, "One kid didn't come back to Bayside – I'm not sure he is going to make it. I expect to see him some day in San Quentin." John said the kid hardly had a chance. "He had a horrible life. Some of these so-called parents – they are biological and that's it. They are on drugs and they are on booze."

Jeanne Elliott says John comes to the school two times a week in the afternoon to help students and organize the mentors for STEM students. When John had his stroke, within two months he returned to this work, uncomplaining, and was helping the middle school students again. "He especially decries the loss of proper grammar and the limited writing skills of the now generation. He defends Latin and all language proper ... yet he is cool."

John has been doing Rotary scholarship interviews for twenty-five years and says that way back then "it was all boys and a sprinkling of girls. And a girl would never say she was interested in math or science." He says that now you read in the *San Mateo Daily Journal* about featured high school kids, including girls, going into engineering and math – it is a whole different world.

John says that when they did the last Rotary student scholarship interviews at Abbott Middle School there were twenty-seven eighth graders who applied – twenty-five girls and two boys. John's favorite line is that "the male of the species is slowly getting run over and they don't know it is happening."

John wonders how much school districts are driven by socioeconomic considerations. John has lived through four or five school superintendents. He says, "**Superintendent Rick Damelio** was serious about taking care of people." But in general, he says the people on the west side of town control the city schools and "that's where all the resources go. You go to a school Board of Trustees meeting and who is doing all the talking? Is it anybody from the poor east side of town? Who represents them? There seems to be no energy toward making things change."

John says that as director of Samaritan House, with his "buddy" Principal Evelyn Taylor, they provided east-side North Shoreview School $10,000 a year for "extras." He says that amount was a drop in the bucket compared to what west side schools like Baywood and others have "where the PTA or PTSA can do all that extra stuff. If we didn't help, the North Shoreview kids wouldn't have anything." He asks why some schools on the west side not have adopted some poor schools on the east side. "There are a lot of things that need to get changed."

In addition to John's direct involvement at Bayside and Abbott middle schools through the Rotary, John is a Board member and an advocate for youth through the Police Activities League (PAL). Even during his Samaritan House days John was helping troubled youth. John worked with Coach **Leroy Miranda** to help him develop a PAL soccer team at San Mateo High School. Leroy says that he and John worked as a team helping former high school gang members choose a different path.

Leroy had a Mexican dad and a Native American Cherokee and white mom. He was raised first in a white and then in a black environment when he was bussed to Hunters Point for fourth, fifth and sixth grades. Leroy fought his way through a school where he was racially the odd kid out. Transferred again to the San Francisco Outer Mission, Leroy got into sports to channel his tendency to get in trouble. Using his high energy for sports led him to mingle with other nationalities. "After a while color wasn't an issue. We bonded and I realized I could go somewhere through sports (wrestling and soccer)."

At nineteen Leroy dabbled in semipro soccer in Los Angeles but injury ended his thoughts of going pro. But he still plays soccer now at age fifty-one. Through sports he met **Mike Buckle** of the San Mateo Police Department and Leroy got his seven-year-old son into the PAL judo program. Leroy helped Mike with the kids and Mike asked if Leroy would like to coach a team of troubled, at-risk youths. These kids were gangbangers – Norteños and Sureños or likely to become members of these gangs. Mike told Leroy that he had encountered kids in San Mateo High School who were lost and looking for a way out of the gangs. Leroy agreed to coach and the two men took eleven decidedly wary and suspicious fifteen to seventeen year old kids on a hike to get acquainted. The group of eleven grew to eighteen as they began rudimentary soccer lessons and practice.

Mike Buckle suggested that PAL Board member John Kelly might help Leroy. It turns out that John had been watching the soccer activity for a few weeks and Leroy had noticed "this tall, old gentleman" on the sidelines. John introduced himself as knowing nothing about soccer but said he would watch for a while. So while Leroy was teaching soccer and conditioning and teamwork, John was beginning to find an angle to help the kids "find their inner selves" and a way to "motivate them" to learn and improve.

When Leroy first talked to these soccer kids he said John naively asked how many of them had a Social Security card. They laughed at him. More than half of them were not born here. Say what you want about immigration but if you have spent some time dealing with these kids, as John has, you end up loving them. You realize how good they are and what potential they have. Leroy told John that "the kids didn't want to read and they couldn't write in English or Spanish." John was especially concerned about the kids' poor school background and offered a room at nearby Samaritan House to "teach them how to read!"

John had simple books for the kids to read but they could barely make it through a sentence and the others made fun of the mistakes. At first John and Leroy could only hold their attention for fifteen minutes but then Leroy began bringing snacks. "If you feed them they will come." And they did come.

One day Leroy wound up with a potential gang war with seventeen of his boys and twelve or so of the opposition gang in the middle of Poplar Avenue ready to rumble. His kids trusted Coach Leroy and backed off when the police made an appearance. Leroy thanked his kids and asked that he be given a heads-up when something happens during the day so they could be prepared. The kids in turn apologized and said they should have warned Leroy. At the next Samaritan House after-session more trust was evident toward Leroy, and soon the kids began calling John "Abuelo" or Grandfather as a sign of respect.

Leroy says, "John is very straightforward; he'll be very honest with you and the kids took to him. John started to get to know some of the boys and they started to put more effort into their work. After about six months the guys would walk over and greet John, 'Abuelo, what's doin'.' They'd tease John about his poor hearing and about John's expression, 'Oh stop it,' eventually buying him a t-shirt with that expression written on the back."

John started following up at school. He knew the **San Mateo High School Principal, Yvonne Shiu,** and would show up periodically during the day to check up on the kids. He'd walk around, talk to the Principal and ask how they were doing. He'd make trips to the library and teach the kids where the Youth Center was so they could find out about college. "Many of these kids had never been in the library, much less a career center." John would push it all the time: "How are your grades? Show me." When a kid got good grades Leroy and John made it a point to let everybody in the group know. "So and so got a B today in English" and everybody would clap. That's when Leroy and John knew things were changing.

The boys were told that soccer was a privilege and if they did well in school and on the field they would be put in a league. But Leroy told them that they were "still raw and not ready yet for league soccer." Leroy did not want to put them in a situation where they would fail because he feared they would revert back to old gang habits. Meanwhile John would ask them, "Is your homework done?" They'd hem and haw and John would say, "No excuses, I want to see it."

Leroy says, "At one time I had twenty-six boys but two went to jail, one got shot, and three just walked away from the program." Leroy told them it was an open door program and that they could leave at any time and he would wish them luck. And if they wanted to come back he and John would be there to welcome them back. "At the end of the year we had eighteen boys. At the beginning a couple of boys had a grade point average of under 1.0 meaning they'd rarely show up for class. Principal Yvonne Shiu commented to John how some of those boys had actually "raised their grade point averages to 2.5 and were showing up for class." The police officers driving down the street would now get a wave from these kids instead of the kids turning their backs.

Leroy said a couple of kids did get into trouble and that was expected. "You're not going to keep going uphill all the time. You are going to hit a valley now and then." But they trusted that they could go to John and Leroy when they were in trouble. Leroy explained that the police can't always be in the kids' corner because "if you break the law, they have a job to do. But we are in your corner because we know you and we think you can do good."

John made a couple of trips to see one kid incarcerated at the County Hillcrest Juvenile Facility. The kid had been in a fight and stabbed another kid with a screwdriver. John counseled that kids may be away from the program but that they were not forgotten. "We're going to stick right by you." Leroy would contact the parents and translate for them. He took the mothers to the Hillcrest court session and translated between lawyers, court and parents. Both Leroy and John would go into court as "the kids' mentors, just to support them." They never told the court that they were in a program because of the possible conflict of interest, recognizing that the kids did break the law.

Leroy says John counseled the kids with stories from San Quentin about young men who've made one mistake and got put away for ten years to life. They are never given a chance. They are deemed "hard cases" and the courts wash their hands of them. The courts either send them back to Mexico or they send them to prison and they never get another chance. "We need to fight for them to get that second chance. These are not bad kids. They were defending themselves. The records show these guys as gangbangers but what the courts don't see is how they've changed; how they are trying to turn their lives around. We need to give that side of the story to the court."

Leroy described John's search for additional ways to help these PAL kids who have gotten in trouble. John asked some of the inmates at San Quentin who were taking courses and getting degrees and who had generally turned it around, to write letters to the PAL kids. Leroy describes these letters as moving and powerful, as the San Quentin inmates shared their thoughts about being in a gang. "They initially thought it was the best life – like being in a family. The gang took care of you. But then the moment they got arrested and thrown in prison, all of a sudden the gang washed their hands of you." Even in prison they have the Norteños and Sureños gangs but it wasn't the same. The inmates said you're on your own and it's a dog-eat-dog world there. There are no advantages in prison to belonging to a gang. What you think you are going to get with a gang you don't get. There's no love there. "If you are not banging for the group or selling drugs or killing somebody when you are told to, you are useless to them. This isn't a life for anybody."

Leroy relates that one young man's eyes were watery as he read the story of a San Quentin man who went into prison for murder on the day his son was born. This PAL kid "was born out of wedlock and didn't ever have a father figure." He now has a kid of his own and is a great father. He is currently in college doing quite well. He still calls Leroy on Father's Day to say "Hi Coach. How's John?" And he calls John and asks how Leroy is. The PAL kids would take turns reading these letters out loud to the group. "It was powerful to watch these young men get a reality check from these letters." (See Appendix A)

Some of these young men's parents are in the gardening business which Leroy calls "an honest job." John and Leroy understand that these kids are helping in their folks' businesses on weekends. But they ask the kids, "Is that what you aspire to be – a gardener for the rest of your life? No? I don't think your parents do either." Leroy tells them that the work is respectable and that he admires their parents for their hard work. The mothers frequently do house work and maid service. "But do you really think that's what your folks want you to be? They brought you to the United States to fulfill your dream as a maid or a gardener or a janitor? So show them that you will take it to the next level. Get your education. Walk across that graduation stage."

John tells these kids that if they walk across that stage he'll walk with them. He'll sing if they want him to. John says, "I'll do whatever it takes to get you to walk across that graduation stage." And it often works. PAL honored two of these students because they changed their grades from under 2.0. One went to almost 4.0 and the other was at 3.5. "They were a total reversal of what they were before. They could hold a conversation. They would look you in the eye, smile and converse with you. They'd ask how you were. They even knew how to treat a girl."

The initial behavior trait that really irked John was when girls would walk by the group, the guys would, 'hey, hey, hey' them and whistle. John would ask, "What are you doing? They are not dogs. You want to talk to the young lady, go talk to her. Show her respect. Do you really think a girl is going to come over when you are whistling at her? No – go talk to her. You want a date? Treat them the way you'd want your sister or mother to be treated." Over time some of the guys started getting dates. Leroy says he and John get along so well because their core values are the same: "Respect is key with us."

Success for PAL kids playing soccer came in baby steps. Leroy was coaching a San Bruno league team at the same time he coached the PAL kids. One of the first PAL practice games was against this other team. Leroy huddled both teams, introduced them and told them to just have fun out there, to have a good time. Show some respect. He told both teams, "You know what I expect from you." The PAL team got "shellacked" six to nothing when Leroy called the game. But the PAL guys learned that they did not like to lose and they knew that they could be better. John talked to some of the PAL boys later and they were angry. John told them, "Good, now you know what it takes to win. You lost today. Get over it." They accepted it.

The following week playing a South San Francisco team they tied two to two. Leroy told them they played hard but didn't finish. Three more practice games were played and the PAL guys, playing like a team, won them all. Coach Leroy said he knew the spirit had changed when the kids would beat him to practice. Now they were ready to work. They were seeing that what Leroy and John were preaching actually would work for them on the soccer field and in the classroom.

At this stage the boys had left Samaritan House and were in regular high school classrooms. The principal approved and the janitor would unlock the rooms after regular school hours. Now they were doing regular school work, making sentences on the board, reading the prison letters and news articles about education that John would bring in. Then they would write paragraphs. "You could see how a great cloud was leaving them. You could see it in the way they walked, the way they presented themselves. They were feeling more confident." That's when Leroy knew it was time to let them play in a league.

Leroy scheduled one more game against his San Bruno team that the PAL kids had lost the first practice game to. He scheduled it on the San Mateo High School soccer field so the PAL team could feel like it was a home game. The PAL team wore brand-new uniforms and they were told to invite all their family and friends. Leroy saw only a couple moms, a couple girl friends and a couple sisters and he learned the reality when the kids told him that all the others invited "had to work." John and Leroy realized that some of these parents were working two or three jobs to support their families. So Leroy and John were their family and their fans and their support system all in one.

The San Bruno team scored first but energized the PAL team and the PAL team won four to two. "It was like the weight of the world came off the PAL players. They knew they'd made it." Leroy said his San Bruno team had won two championships and were defending champions that year. Five weeks had transpired since they'd badly beaten the PAL guys so they knew the progress the PAL team had made. So the San Bruno team came over and they all hugged. "It was great to see these ex-gangbangers sit with young men they didn't know and talk after the game." Leroy figured they were ready and they joined a league. The first year they took second place. The second year the PAL team tied for first place.

Four of the boys graduated that June and they invited John and Leroy to their graduation. One kid said there were limited tickets and his father couldn't be there so he wanted John and Leroy to be there in his stead. Of course they accepted. "It was almost like our own sons were walking across the stage." A week later they took the graduates to dinner. The first words out of John's mouth were, "Anybody sign up for college?" And three of them did and one was undecided. John warned he would keep pestering the undecided one and that he wasn't going away. A couple of other guys were a few credits short so John encouraged them to sign up for Adult School to get their GED and keep going. For one of the boys, John went to his house and picked him up and walked him right in to make sure he was registered for classes and warned that he'd be checking on him. And he did check. He stuck with him.

One August day PAL team member **Antonio Escovedo's** mom came to soccer practice and personally thanked Leroy and John. She said, "My son comes home now every day after school. I used to worry because he wouldn't come home until ten or eleven o'clock at night. I knew what he was doing, he was out there with a gang. Now he comes home after soccer practice every day and the first thing he does is ask, 'Mom, what can I help with?' Or if he saw dishes he'd go wash dishes. He'd help his little brother and sister with their homework." She said, "I want to thank you two. He talks about you all the time." In gratitude she brought John and Leroy fresh tamales and presented them right there on the field along with a nice hug. John and Leroy agree that this is what it is all about. That incident was reward enough for everything they had tackled that year.

By the third year both Leroy and John noticed that the PAL guys weren't looking over their shoulders any more like they did when they first came to play. They were not concerned about their former gangs or even the rival gangs. And the gangs were leaving them alone. Coach and John then knew that they were on the right path. When the team members were asked to do something they would do it without hesitation. They'd ask the guys to write a paragraph and they would do it and not question why. John had told the guys that he had been the Dean of Students at Serra High School and met a lot of great young men, "but you know what, there are no greater young men than the ones I see right here in this PAL group. No one has had to work harder and show greater self control and effort than you guys have. I'm proud of you guys – better yet, you guys should be proud of each other."

Leroy says he eventually wore himself out and had a minor stroke, perhaps from his extraordinary effort and focus on his family, job and coaching. He was really touched when five of the PAL team members showed up to see him at his house, with flowers yet. They were worried about him. Their visit brought Leroy to tears. Six or seven years ago these guys would not have given him the time of day. "Now they were here at my front door because they were worried about me."

When John had his stroke in December of 2011, and because of his age and because his was more serious, the kids were really worried. Leroy told them where John was recuperating in a nursing facility in San Mateo and a couple of them went there at first. Then Leroy arranged a van and fourteen boys went to see John. John was moved and wanted so much to sit up and show them he was still their strong leader. They all noticed that John had maybe twenty boxes of candy by the side of his bed, obviously brought by visitors. John said he didn't know what to do with it all. "You guys want a piece?" Picture piranha: the boys dug into the candy.

The guys were really concerned about John and a few days later several of the guys just came back to visit him on their own. And when they found out that John was to be moved out of his second story apartment they jumped at the chance to help. In fact eleven of the boys showed up as part of a large volunteer moving crew to pack up and move John's things from his apartment.

As soon as he could John would have someone drive him back to the practice field and Leroy describes John as the "Pied Piper. All the boys would congregate around John and his walker asking how he was." John would respond by asking them how they were doing in the classroom. And John noticed a lot of new faces on the field and the guys said, "Yeah, that's my little brother; that's my cousin." The PAL guys believed so much in the program that they were bringing their younger siblings. John said, "I'm going to keep coming out here and don't think just because I'm on a walker that I'm not going to be checking up." The group had moved from San Mateo High School to the King Center to make it more convenient for John and the boys. Leroy explains, "John was not about to let what happened to him deter him from helping these kids find themselves."

Even some kids out of the program and now at college came back just to see John. Leroy says, "It just goes to show the love they have for this man and how they cared for what he did for them." Leroy calls John Batman and he is sidekick Robin. He says, "You lead by example. You are a born leader and I see that. John is motivated to help people regardless of his own health. If there is someone out there who could use his help or inspiration, John will be there for him."

John gets a whole table each year at the PAL fund raising awards dinner so that he can bring some of these kids and introduce them to an environment they never see. They get to see people who give money but who more importantly care about the program and who want to meet the kids in the program. One year as the kids were getting ready to leave the dinner there was music playing and the kids were kind of hopping around and some ladies asked if they'd like to dance. Sure enough, as people were starting to leave they were dancing right in the middle of the place; three of the boys and three women who were showing them how to dance. They got such a kick out of that. John said, "See, these people want to meet you. Open up and talk to people. People will help and people do care. It is not just about the money."

Leroy said that when the PAL team won their first championship it was before the biggest audience ever to watch them play. Most of those people were from the PAL Board or were friends of board members. They made up a bigger group even than family members and friends of the team. They had a barbecue right afterwards and the boys felt like celebrities talking about the game and school with people they had never met. John would walk by and say, "Tell them about the B you got on that paper the other day." And, "Talk to this one who hasn't signed up for college yet." The kids don't mind John's prodding because they know he really cares.

Leroy talks about a Korean kid named **Dook** in the program. "When he joined us he was a lost individual with no sense of direction." Dook knew a couple of the boys who had been in the program for two years and they encouraged him to come out and just have fun. The kid was reluctant and said that he didn't know how to play soccer. He did come out but couldn't look Leroy in the eye much less the substantially taller John. John asked him how he was doing in school and he hemmed and hawed. John asked him to bring him his report card. Leroy gave the kid Leroy's own soccer shoes and taught him to play soccer. John, meanwhile, took him to the Career Center and got him a tutor. Dook went to tutoring and John would check on him. By his senior year he was taking Spanish and could read and speak it. In addition to his native Korean he began taking French. He had turned all his grades around and at graduation in 2010 they asked him to speak. He gave a very moving speech; he thanked the PAL Program; he thanked Leroy. He especially thanked John for motivating him and making him feel special like a man who could do whatever he wanted. He said that he was lost and didn't know what he wanted to do but "now I know that I am somebody." He brought the audience to tears and they stood up and gave him a standing ovation. Dook is now at College of San Mateo and interested in a mentoring program.

Leroy adds that Police Chief Manheimer is the backbone of the program and that she truly believes in the program and the work that John does. "She gave us carte blanche." One year John realized that these kids always lack school supplies. "Why don't we get them supplies – I'll give you money." Leroy suggested they pitch it back to the Police Department because they have a budget for such things and he and John could do the shopping. "The Chief jumped on it right away and said sure, whatever they need." So Leroy and John bought pencils, backpacks, paper, calculators and all the normal school supplies they would need. They put the supplies into backpacks and distributed them to those kids who signed up for them. Later they would come up to John with pride and say, "See John, I've got my backpack with me." And John would answer, "Yeah, but is your homework in there? Show me."

Leroy says, "John knows how to push the right buttons and yet knows how to back off, when to listen and most of all when to be the driving force. He's first gear; he takes you out of neutral, puts you in first and shows you the direction and makes sure you shift into second and third. That's John."

The Police Activities League is sponsored by the City of San Mateo and run by Chief of Police Manheimer. She invited John to join the PAL Board and expected him to be like other Board of Directors members and with his contacts raise some money and talk about PAL programs in the community. She says John Kelly's role turned out to be much more than just a Board member. She knew John mentored and coached at many different schools. He focused on youths who were challenged or big trouble including those incarcerated at Hillcrest Juvenile Facility. So she talked to him about her vision of the Police Activities League turning from a prevention program for all kids, to really directing and focusing on those youth who already had been first time offenders and were in gangs. "I knew I had him hooked." She never expected that bringing John Kelly in to work with PAL would gain them "such a critical role model, mentor, advocate and trusted ally for our troubled youth."

John has been there "when all of us have wrung our hands and said we just can no longer deal with a youth." Even when kids have gotten into serious trouble John has mentored and tutored them and said, "That's OK, we won't forget about you." He has stayed in touch with their families. Susan says that what John does is "so not for recognition. He does it because it is the right and important thing to do." He intuitively and instinctively knows what the "needs of needy people are; that includes me at times. When I've been so downhearted about a kid we've worked so hard with – he'll notice that and come to me and minister to my needs, while also being mindful of the kid."

Susan sees John as a parent to everybody; one who believes in unconditional love. "Something you can't fake. It truly comes from the spirit and heart." She thinks it comes through so clearly that kids especially, who can sense the BS, automatically turn to him when they are in need. "His unconditional love is more than a cop's love; sometimes it is more than a coach's love." She says though sometimes what is needed is tough love and she's not sure John is capable of tough love. But she adds that "there always has to be the one unconditional loving grandparent around. And that is John for our entire community." No matter how successful and accomplished you are or how dire in need you are in a prison, in a youth group, in Juvenile Hall or just dropping out of the programs that are going to help you, "John's complete unconditional love soothes all of those savage demons among people." She has seen him just work miracles.

Susan gets crosswise at times with John because she's "going to put limits on. I'm the parent who is going to do the tough love and make sure this kid is out of the gang and make sure there are consequences." She thinks John is not there for the consequences; that John is there just to be their advocate. And that *is* part of the PAL youth development model. "Everyone's got to have that grandparent. Our society is truly missing its grandparents." She says that grandparents give unconditional love and let you know that no matter how bad things are, you're going to be OK. She thinks if we had more of those grandparents around there would be less dysfunction in our society.

The Police Activities Program tries to "incent kids with the carrot and the stick." She says if they want to play rugby or soccer or tap dance or volleyball "that's great but here's your social contract. You need to get out of the gangs. You need to get back to school. You need to improve your grades." She says it works but sometimes it is "two steps forward and one step back." For these kids who have had multiple generations of family members as bad influences it takes a long time. Well, insert John Kelly in there and he just has them progress by leaps and bounds solely through love and understanding. It's almost like an "inoculation" and you can't give it any other way. "There is only one John Kelly vaccine." He builds kids' self confidence by saying, "Whatever it is that you've done, there is a reason and purpose and a highest calling for you. Let's find it and let's get there."

John pretty much is the grandfather for the whole PAL soccer team. They took a group of young Sureños from San Mateo High School and the PAL school resource officer told them they can't be doing the gang stuff anymore. He warned they were going to get hurt and that their younger brothers and sisters were watching them. He said, don't perpetuate the cycle of violence and asked what they wanted to do instead. PAL said they were "going to invest in you. What do you want to do?" And they all wanted to play soccer. But because their grades were bad and they had not attended well they were trouble in school. The school would not let them on the school soccer team. These gang members really didn't have a focus to do much of anything.

PAL proposed a social contract with this gang and if they agreed to get out of the gang and become the PAL gang, "we will invest in you. We will provide you fields. We will get you in a soccer league, we will provide you uniforms." They found Leroy to coach. He was a professional soccer player and the parent of one of the kids. Susan described him as this young dashing soccer star and says they are in awe of him. These kids in gangs are looking to follow and be part of something important and something exclusive. And that something for this Sureño group was soccer. They began working out on a hard scrabble field. "You don't want to give them everything. They need to earn it."

Leroy Miranda, the soccer coach, found he needed something more for these kids. PAL didn't know where to find the mentors for them. They needed someone who would be able to speak their language, who would really be able to work with them. Susan says, "Son of a gun, we were just talking about it in our PAL Board meeting (maybe six years ago) and John spoke up and said, 'I'll do it.'" Susan didn't know John that well yet and she looked at him as "this sixty-five, maybe seventy-year-old white guy, kind of teetering on his cane, wanting to hang with the San Mateo Sureños and be relevant to them and to coach them." And she was thinking he was a well-meaning PAL Board member. But at that time she didn't know the magic of John Kelly. John did get involved and it is very strange to Susan how those boys started hanging on him. "When he'd be around they would just orbit him."

When a couple of the kids got in trouble and were up at Hillcrest Juvenile Hall "we had some pretty hard discussions. Do you let them go? Do you hang on to them? They clearly hadn't gotten out of the gang. So we had to show consequences because we were trying to break the gang." Susan and John disagreed because "John is going to save them and be their lion father and grandfather and I want the consequences."

Susan has also gotten crosswise with John regarding certain community members. John has advocated for some folks who Susan believes "have continued to be bad citizens and need to have consequences." Susan says, though, that she can talk very frankly with John. And John will listen and he will weigh what you say and then give you what he feels is the right answer "based on the strongest moral and spiritual compass that I've ever seen. And he is unflappable." Susan says she'll reason with him: "this guy has to go; he's bad; he's doing drugs. And John will not care. He's that father lion who defends his cubs at all costs." Susan says the truth is it is good to be in John's lair because then you have an advocate for life. You can't buy that; you can't emulate it. You either have it… and he intrinsically has it. Susan thinks that's what so amazing about John Kelly. She thinks her anger is more directed at the fact that "he is right in a lot of ways but society has to move on sometimes in the real world.

"I honor him and I am extremely grateful that he has chosen to take the kids who are really our toughest nuts to crack and recognize that we must do something early with them." Otherwise they'll end up as San Quentin ex-cons who are valiantly struggling and often fail to get out of that cycle of violence.

Susan thinks the ways in which she is sometimes exasperated with John are exactly the things we need him around for. He challenges us all to make sure that what we are doing is right on behalf of humanity. And he always brings us back to that. She thinks we are blessed to have John around and that the kids know that instinctively. "He has a real magical power with kids."

John followed up with one of those kids in serious trouble and actually brought the family to Hillcrest. They had not really been involved. That kid graduated high school which he had no hopes of doing prior to the PAL soccer team and John Kelly. He later got into CSM Community College and became a mentor for the younger kids. Now he is a young father, has a good job and his mother, who was interviewed in tears, said "I've never known this son. He is such a wonderful son. That's really the power of John Kelly." Susan credits the program and the wonderful soccer coach but "it was John Kelly who really started showing this kid that no one is a throw-away; no one is going to be dropped. You have a place in this world and we're going to show you that place." John Kelly to Susan is the "outward action of what we say we are going to do. We are going to invest in our youth, but you know what, we can do all the programs in the world. But until you touch a kid's heart and soul and let them know they have unconditional love you don't really get there."

Susan says that there is story after story of the forty or so youth that he has touched through the soccer team. Now when he gets honored in our community there are always soccer kids coming by to honor him.

The kids do remember and appreciate John. Leroy said that on a recent Monday night he and John went out to dinner with one of their original soccer team members and his girl friend. This young man had just turned twenty-one and had his life totally together. He's working full time and he not only resists the urge to get in trouble but helps other kids to not do what he did. Being involved in PAL with attention from John really made a huge difference.

John says there is a principle of restorative justice in that all of us are responsible for developing a climate in our community where "we can counteract what influences people into criminal behavior. And there are all kinds of opportunities and chances."

Nine

Restorative Justice

John entered the big house, California State Prison San Quentin for the first time and thought, so this is what prison life is like. John felt a bit apprehensive as the massive metal-barred gate clanked shut behind him. Guests and guards both pass through ID control points and into an entry cell controlled by the uniformed gate keeper behind bullet proof glass. Once inside the entry cell he saw steel bars ahead and the steel gate locked him in from behind. John was now entirely controlled and contained by an anonymous guard barely visible through the raised, thick glass enclosure. Temporarily, he too was now an inmate.

Passing though the sally port John remembered the warden's briefing: "You are on your own if you are taken prisoner; we don't bargain for or rescue hostages." He thought anxiously, "What was I thinking? What am I doing here? Of my own accord I am walking into the classic den of murderers and thieves. I have no protection. I must be crazy."

John showed his guest pass to the obscured guard and the inner steel gate opened. He passed down a dingy entryway into the gray of an enclosed central yard. He was now locked in a notorious prison and distinguished from the permanent residents only by his clothes which were not blue. 'Guys in blue' is the vernacular for prisoners dressed in many shades of blue denim – shirts, pants and jackets.

John Kelly has been interested in social and restorative justice his whole adult life. Since John retired as director of Samaritan House he has been ever more involved with helping and guiding men who are in prison or have spent time in prison or in the California Youth Authority. John travels the one hour plus to San Quentin Prison to conduct programs like Kairos as often as three times a week. At last count there were seventy self-help programs at San Quentin. Kairos and two or three others are the most effective. I've talked to guys who have told me that John and Kairos have turned their lives around.

Why should anyone be concerned about restorative justice? Many believe public safety requires that we lock up criminals and "throw away the key." The fact is that all but a few inmates are eventually released back into our communities. So aside from moral grounds, our safety and well being are best served by helping convicted felons restore themselves prior to and after their release.

The following is a description of restorative justice taken from the

Tom Huening

Christian-based Prison Fellowship. (http://www.justicefellowship.org, or http://en.wikipedia.org/wiki/Restorative_justice)

<u>What is Restorative Justice?</u>
Restorative Justice is a practical, biblical approach to the problems of crime and punishment in our society. While it has foundations in the Old and New Testaments, it is not just a Christian concept. Restorative justice is indigenous to many cultures around the world and has been practiced for millennia.

The principles of restorative justice are simple. Restorative justice recognizes that crime harms people. It does not simply break a law. The justice system should aim to repair these injuries. Crime is also more than a matter between the government and an individual offender. Since crime victims and the community bear the brunt of crime, they, too, must be actively involved in the criminal justice process.

<u>Restoring Victims</u>
There's a huge difference between justice that punishes and justice that restores. The injuries that crime victims experience are significant; crime may disrupt their lives temporarily, or for as long as they live. What's more, many victims feel re-victimized by the criminal justice system itself, especially when it excludes them from much of the process.

Restorative justice promotes the need for victims' concerns to be considered in every part of the criminal justice process. Victims need help regaining a sense of control over their lives, and they need restitution to compensate for some amount of their loss.

<u>Restoring Offenders</u>
Restorative justice requires the system to do more than warehouse offenders. Restorative justice means holding offenders personally accountable. They need to confront the pain they have caused their victims and take the steps necessary to overcome their criminal behavior.

Restorative justice also means delivering punishments to offenders that are proportional to the harm they committed. It means offering offenders opportunities for rehabilitation. And it means treating offenders with fairness and dignity, even when they are locked behind bars.

Restoring Communities

Crime injures the community, as well. It erodes public safety and confidence, disrupts order, and undermines common values. Our response to crime must consider these harms.

Governments should give communities an integral role in helping offenders re-enter society and in restoring peace. Communities should also take responsibility to support victims and help them reorder their lives. And, they should care for the families of offenders during their time of need.

Disregarding any of these areas short-circuits our criminal justice system.

Restorative Justice in Action

We can fulfill the principles of restorative justice with policies that:

Make available victim-offender mediation sessions

Create diversion programs that move nonviolent, minimal-risk offenders out of prison and into community-based treatment

Offer re-entry preparation for offenders anticipating release

Remove barriers to offenders' successful reintegration into society – such as restrictions on residency or employment that are not necessary to protect public safety

Modify prison sentence lengths to justly reflect the harm caused by the crime committed

Protect offenders from violence while they are in prison

Strengthen the families of offenders

Increase opportunities for prisoners' transformation by protecting their religious freedom and their access to mentoring relationships

We have suffered decades of failures in criminal justice. It is time to turn to what may seem a new and radical model but is actually a long-standing and well-proven one: justice that restores.

Patrick Kelly, John's nephew, the son of his deceased brother **Michael** and Michael's (living) wife **Barbara** provides a good introduction to John's focus on restorative justice. He sometimes accompanies John on his trips to San Quentin.

Patrick says that John is a huge believer in restorative justice and that John is "incredibly jazzed" after a San Quentin restorative justice session. Many inmates are like sons and look to him for guidance. He is a constant in their lives and gives them an opportunity to have a dialogue about important things.

Whenever John goes to San Quentin or to a more exclusive outside event, he says that he feels more comfortable in San Quentin than with local wealthy people. The people in San Quentin are his friends and look up to him. They all have done something wrong and know it. They understand that they are paying the price but "in some cases the price is beyond what it should be."

Patrick talks to inmate **Michael** from the Kid C.A.T. club every time he visits. "He is incredibly bright and charismatic. As a teenager he was in the wrong place at the wrong time, perhaps only driving a car when a friend committed murder." Once convicted, he was locked up and the key was thrown away. The normal societal reaction is that this is a "horrible, horrible person who can never change; a gang-banger in prison – lock him away for life."

(The Kid C.A.T. club stands for Kids Creating Awareness Together. It is a club for inmates in San Quentin who are serving a life sentence for crimes committed before they were eighteen. More at *San Quentin News*, June 2011 edition.)

When Patrick meets these inmates who are friends of John he sees that they have come to terms with their crimes and who they are as a person. He can see why John has this passion. "How many of us didn't do something wrong as a teenager?" Patrick says there are degrees of wrong, but a lot has to do with a youthful burst of testosterone. It seems unfair not to give any of them a second chance for a life. Patrick has changed how he thinks about it thanks to John and meeting these "real people." He is sure there are some who should stay locked up. There is something really wrong in the extreme Charles Manson type but not many fit that category. Patrick says that without John he would not have seen or experienced that.

John says he started down the road to restorative justice during the last five years that he was a priest by participating in a Cursillo program. While he was at St. Mark's Parish there were many folks who were making this Cursillo retreat and John's initial attitude was, "That's for lay people and I'm a priest – I don't need that." The organizers were always trying to get priests to be directors for the program but most priests were like John and thought they didn't need it. But they finally convinced John to attend and he described it as "an unbelievable experience."

Cursillo, as mentioned earlier, is a small course, comparable to Kairos but outside of prison. It starts Friday night and goes for three full days. It is described as people coming together in retreat fashion to share what it means to be Christian. It has the same kind of intensity and the talks are somewhat comparable to Kairos.

Jerry Forbes got John into an original Cursillo retreat by "just beating him up." John, as priest, thought he had learned all that was taught at Cursillo but he liked it anyway and wound up getting involved. But Jerry says that "Kairos, the prison form of Cursillo, was John's real calling. He loves it." Jerry jokes, "John fits in with those people and maybe with John's past indiscretions he is actually serving his time there at San Quentin."

From John's first retreat in 1976 until he left the priesthood three years later, John was always on a Cursillo team. But John told the Cursillo folks, "You don't need us priests, just go ahead and do it – you lay people have more sense than we do." A local guy, **John Carberry**, happened to be the leader of a Cursillo John made.

After John stopped being a priest in 1979 he said he was basically ignored – "nobody even bothered with me." But in 1991 John Carberry asked if Vic Perrella and John wanted to make a Kairos. John asked, "What in the world is that?" And Carberry explained that it was a Cursillo retreat but inside a prison. It was a weekend of spirituality; literally, God's Special Time. John's first reaction was, "What the hell do I want to go into a prison for? That is the last place on the face of the earth I want to be." Vic and John Kelly both thought the request was insane. But after they first attended the weekend they were "so bloody hooked" that they "couldn't resist being in there, in San Quentin." And as a result John Kelly and Vic Perrella are, still today, in the prison two or three times a week.

John explains that, "The original history of Kairos was to deal with lifers and set up a system where they could learn how to help each other inside after we left." These were people who were going to be around for a long, long time. At San Quentin it gradually went from not only lifers but also short termers. John says there is a huge gap between lifers and short termers. With the lifers, a lot of them will come into their prison setting and will still be the same person they were before they got there – still playing games, contra-banding drugs. But usually after five or ten years something dawns: They don't feel good, don't feel alive, don't feel human. Something has to be different. Gradually they start to want to take a deeper look at what it means "to be a human being. And once that happens ...."

Tom Huening

John says for the first few San Quentin Kairos they struggled to get the guys in blue (inmates) to take it seriously. They'd walk in on a Friday night wondering, what the hell am I doing here? Why am I wasting my time? Then the Kairos team would watch the change that takes place over the four days. Now so many men have participated in this and other self-help programs, it's easy to get inmates. "We now have a waiting list because the word is out; it is now the thing to do." Other than the outside guys (volunteers), the major influence is the lifers inside who have recruited these guys and trained them to take it seriously. A nucleus of guys in San Quentin lend their support and commit to helping other prisoners.

On Saturday the week before they went in for their first Kairos, John's team went inside to meet the team who were going to be working with them. At first John was apprehensive but he came to realize that the San Quentin façade looked just like his seminary building. Soon he felt right at home.

John said that at every Kairos weekend there are maybe ten inside guys who have already made Kairos who spend the whole weekend waiting on everybody. They bring things to the table; they work to make sure everything is functioning correctly; they are called the "inside team." Their commitment over that weekend is impressive. John says for the guys inside to see the unbelievable sharing that this inside team does is a profound lesson for them.

(Some 2012 facts about the Kairos Organization: They say they have 36,000 volunteers contributing more than three million hours of service in over four hundred institutions around the world. "Each year over 25,000 inmates and their family members are introduced to God's love, grace and forgiveness through Kairos." kpmifoundation.org)

John summarizes the San Quentin Kairos as "a Christian based weekend with an intense sharing of time, energy and love with one another." Worldwide Kairos has a California state council and a local council that sets up programs and recruits people to make it work. John is the leader of a core group of guys who have done Kairos. There have been forty-one Kairos at San Quentin and John has made thirty-four of them. He began with Kairos number four and only missed Kairos thirty-nine because of his stroke. But he then made Kairos forty on 2012 Labor Day weekend and Kairos forty-one in February 2013.

Some two thousand inmates have made this weekend. John explains that the inside guys can have visitors only on Sunday morning; the rest of the days they have to commit to the program and forgo visitors. The most significant feedback John and his team get every time about the Kairos weekend is, "This is the event that changed my life." John says you can just see it happen.

John says it is not unusual to have three or four Muslims and maybe a couple of Jews and "when we present Jesus up front to that group everybody is all OK with it." John had one Muslim tell him at the end of one session that he had respect for Jesus and that "I'm a better Muslim now because I made Kairos. It is the same truth."

John just loves that he is a buddy with a lot of the Muslims and with a lot of the Protestants and with a lot of the Catholics in the building. John gets along with just about every group "because we are talking the same language."

When he goes there on Sunday he goes to the Protestant chapel at 10:30 and stays for about forty-five minutes while they are singing. Then he goes to the Catholic chapel for the rest of the Mass, usually at the sermon. So he does both. He says he probably has more friends in the Protestant chapel than the Catholic because more of them are Kairos graduates. John says the Protestant community is two-thirds black and in that place "I don't even recognize color – it is not even an issue. And it is not an issue for them. We are just friends. We get along fabulously well." The Catholic service is whites and Hispanics primarily; there are a few blacks who sneak in. John asks black Catholics he meets at San Quentin if their family is from Louisiana. "Ninety-nine percent of the time they are."

John describes the mechanics of the Kairos weekend as forty-two inside guys (prisoners) and thirty-five or so outside guys (volunteers) who mostly are Catholic and Protestant of different denominations and degrees of affiliation with their church. The volunteers are just people committed to what Jesus is about. John says, he doesn't agree with all of them – there are some "fundamentalists," but when they get together in this setting it is a "whole new world." It is just people sharing with people and "showing real support and love. The effect is overwhelming."

They start Kairos on Friday night and go until Monday night and have a series of talks and meditations that guys on the outside give in a structured format. They divide the group into tables of six inside guys and three or four outside guys. They sit at the same table for all three days, and at the end of each talk spend maybe fifteen or twenty minutes finding out what the talk meant to everybody. On Friday night there are meditations, not talks, because it is more about reflecting on what is said. "Know Yourself" is a session about who are you really as a human being and what part are you leaving out and not paying attention to and how did you get here. And "Prodigal Son" is, no matter how bad you think you are, you can come back.

John says day one is a "Who am I" type of talk. The second day is focused more on forgiveness and the third day is focused on how do I effect change in my own life – either here or someplace else (after release). One of John's favorite sessions on Saturday morning is "Choices": no matter how many people you want to blame for why you are here, you made the choices and you can change them. That is, "you have the power to change."

There is an associated Kairos movement called "You Are Not Alone" where people all over on the outside are praying for the inside group every hour of every day while it is going on. They have posters that people on the outside have written messages on and they hang them up on the prison room wall. And they have music. Of the thirty-five or so outside guys three or four are musicians, guitar players, mostly folk stuff.

The Kairos team usually stays overnight outside at the nearby Protestant Seminary in San Anselmo when they have room, otherwise at a motel. There are six or so ladies who support the team on the outside. They have meals ready for when they get home. They are their spiritual support for the weekend.

Jerry Forbes, a regular Kairos team member, explains that of the forty-two inmates typically at a Kairos weekend most have not ever spoken to a group. Most are minorities; many are young "who you know have never talked." Yet they get up and talk about the Kairos experience. "It's enough to make you cry and to make you ask, what the hell happened here?" Jerry says that seeing the change in people has been really good for John and that's why he sticks with Kairos.

John gets the feeling that he is genuinely doing something for somebody who is really down and out. And "that's what John is all about." Jerry is not "into miracles but when I see them happen, whoa!" What the Kairos prisoners really like is that the outsiders keep coming back. Jerry says that when you sign up on a Kairos team you sign up to come back once a month for a year. An inmate told him, "You guys keep coming back, so you really must care." Jerry says a lot of other groups come in, give them a "one shot deal, then never come back."

John says that the Kairos weekend generates a sense of togetherness and family. "By Monday night you wouldn't believe what has transpired." There is one song called The Community Song – it has all kinds of gestures – and when they first start out singing it on Saturday the guys are saying, "What is this crazy deal?" John says that by Monday night "the guys are jumping out in the aisle bouncing around."

One powerful moment is that all of the outside guys write a personal letter to the guys on the inside. On Sunday night when they get back from dinner there is a bag with all these letters and the letters are passed around. The inside guys have no idea that this is coming. And some of the guys just break down. For some of them it is the only letter they've gotten the whole time they've been in prison. They have Kleenex boxes on the table for inmates.

A former inmate said to John, "I bawled my eyes out when I realized the pain and suffering I caused; I just let go more than I had ever let go in my life." John says that this realization is not unusual when inmates get letters from the guys who have already made the Kairos and from other people. They are reading letters addressed to them personally and "all of a sudden they are overwhelmed by the fact that people care about them."

Right after the letters is a birthday party. The outside ladies make this huge cake with everybody's name on it. And they sing happy birthday for "the beginning of the next day of your life. And for some of them it is the only time they've ever had a birthday cake."

On Sunday night they have all the guys, including the outside guys, get a piece of paper and write a list of all the people that they have to forgive; those who have done something bad to them in life. Then they have an "unbelievably beautiful ritual where we have a pot there and couple of candles and the guys bring their paper, light it and put it in the pot to burn their forgiveness lists." There is a powerful effect of each guy taking a new look at his life.

Also on Sunday the guys are asked, OK, what are you going to do about all this? How are you going to change your life? At the end of the day they have them answer three questions: What were you like spiritually when you got here? What has happened to you, what did you learn on the weekend? And, what are you going to do from here?

On Monday night the inside guys think the weekend is over and that the outside guys are about ready to go home. They all go back and forth between the Catholic and Protestant chapels. Then from the Catholic chapel they walk out imagining they are going to say a final prayer. As they walk out of that room all the guys at San Quentin in blue who have made Kairos before form a channel for them to walk through, holding candles and screaming and hollering, congratulating them.

Then they walk into the Protestant chapel and there are usually fifty to a hundred outside people who have come in for the final celebration giving a standing ovation. For John, "It was the most powerful experience I have ever had." The prisoners go up on stage and all answer those three questions. The table families have developed responses to the questions and pick out one representative to report the answers. They get a chance to share what the experience was like for them. In the meantime there are probably a hundred or more guys who have already done Kairos yelling encouragement and jumping up and down. "Oh god, it is.... The very first Kairos I was on, that Monday night I was crying my eyes out. And that got me hooked."

John brought his Bayside School counseling buddy Dick Nelson to a recent final ceremony and Dick was amazed at the love these inmates show for John. He said that all know and greet John and say he is a "fabulous guy." Many inmates have no family that pays any attention so John and their fellow Kairos participants become like family. Dick calls himself a "beginning Christian" and was impressed with "what the love of the Lord had done for this class of forty-two men." He said their "overwhelming enthusiasm rejuvenated and inspired me spiritually."

Vic Perrella, John's Kairos partner, said he and John first met in the Eighties while participating in the Cursillo movement. John and Vic together worked the fourth Kairos in San Quentin in 1991 and from that moment on they were "Kairos junkies." Vic says he thinks he can speak for the both of them in saying they found a type of spirituality among those whom society had forgotten. Probably the most impactful feeling they experienced over time was "the transformational process that these condemned men made in their lives." As one would expect – looking from the outside in – they sensed that society had given up on inmates as individuals. In other words, "free people feel inmates deserve to be there. They will never change, so just throw away the key and let them rot." Change, as much of society perceives it, isn't possible.

Vic says that neither John nor he is a "bible thumper." Their ministry is based on moral and, of course, Christian values. And, "we do believe that change is possible!"

Vic has witnessed that John Kelly possesses a foundational belief that "all men are intrinsically good, that everyone makes mistakes but, with the help of others, will seek changes in their lives if given the opportunity." And as we often hear the expression, "John not only talks the talk but walks the walk."

After John's twenty-five years as a Catholic priest Vic can't imagine the mental and spiritual dislocation he experienced when he decided to leave that life and start a ministry for those in need. How does one leave a life which he thought was fulfilling only to find it was not? This decision was not an easy one. "Thankfully, he did. That step had to be momentous ... and frightening!"

But Samaritan House and John's prison ministry were the result of making that choice which Vic describes as "a legacy now, that those in need will enjoy in the future." How appropriate when you think back to Matthew's 'Beatitudes' and the 'Last Judgment' Bible passages.

Vic says that John truly possesses the virtue of humility and wants no recognition. He says he's filled with joy by helping and being of service to others. And when he thinks of the men who have served twenty to thirty-five years in San Quentin and are now outside, he would have to agree that "there isn't a greater sense of peace and joy! They were not forgotten and they will never forget John." Vic calls John Kelly the "St. Francis of Assisi of the twenty-first century" and says he has been blessed to have been part of John's life.

John says, "In San Quentin what these inmates had to go through to survive their parents is unbelievable. Many were screwed up psychologically and emotionally almost from the day they were born. The biggest thing now is them coming to a realization that there is within them the power to change and to become healthy, on their own."

(Lifers, in prison parlance, are those who have been sentenced to fifteen years or more to life in prison with the possibility of parole. The term does not generally include those who are on death row or those sentenced to life without the possibility of parole).

John says "a perfect example" is this group of nine guys who are in this Kid C.A.T. (Creating Awareness Together) program. John got introduced to this program in 2011. These are guys who have committed serious crimes – usually murder or they were involved with a murder when they were teenagers – and all sent to state facilities. Their whole purpose now is based on the idea that this is not the way to treat a teenager. John says that the last thing we should do is "send a kid who is fourteen or fifteen into an adult prison to spend his life with all these other characters."

These men are now committed to developing a curriculum inside to teach other guys inside to wise up – particularly other teenagers. They are writing a journal and creating a video to convince teens outside not do what they did. They also want to try to find a way to change the official system to find a new way to deal with young offenders. About a month ago there was a major seminar at San Quentin from Thursday afternoon to Saturday addressing these issues – outside people coming in and Kid C.A.T. trying to gain outside support.

One person John lined up to attend was **Senator Leland Yee** because he had a reform bill before the California Senate. He came in and stayed for about two hours. John thinks he was very much moved by what he saw. John is trying to get him to come back in again and sit down and talk with these nine guys who all have made Kairos; they have all also been involved in other self help programs. John sits down with them when he has a chance and "when I come home I say, there is no way I can believe that they did what they did."

John calls the nine some of "finest human beings I have ever met in my life." They are all now in their early thirties. Some are going to the Parole Board for a hearing and all have been there for at least ten to fifteen years. The youngest one was fourteen when he was sentenced to state prison. Leland Yee's point, "which is right on," is that a teenager does not have the same capacity to make decisions the way an adult does and therefore we need to take that into account about the decision that they made to commit their crime. To John, "These guys are all close friends of mine and I love them."

John relates that Senator Yee's strong interest in juvenile justice finally resulted in his bill SB 9 being passed. Yee's bill was signed by Governor Brown on September 30, 2012. It would let the inmates who were juveniles when they committed their crimes ask judges to reconsider their sentences after they serve at least fifteen years in prison. Judges could then reduce a no-parole sentence to twenty-five years-to-life if the inmate shows remorse and is taking steps toward rehabilitation.

Some people think it is criminal that John is dealing with these guys of the Kid C.A.T. program since all of them committed or were involved in a murder. John says, "OK, they did it as teenagers. And I'm supposed to say that we condemn them for the rest of their lives – that there is no chance for them to change?" John listens to the things that they want to do, the message they want to deliver. John says that the people they want to be "are those our society needs." They want to get out and explain to troubled young people why they've got to stay out of gangs and why they need to avoid unlawful behavior to have a decent life. "They are in a better position to teach that lesson than I am."

One of John's favorites is graduation day of the Prison University Project. The project is sponsored by Patten College in the East Bay, a small Christian denomination school that brings volunteers to San Quentin to teach college courses. Each time there are five, ten, fifteen guys graduating with an AA Degree. The inmates are permitted to dress in caps and gowns and they get to invite their families. "It is one of the most beautiful graduations I go to." They also graduate guys who have completed their GED and guys who have gotten certificates in a technical field for eventual outside employment, so there are maybe thirty or forty graduates at these various levels. It is a whole different experience from a graduation outside. And John usually knows a third or half of those graduating. "It is very meaningful for me."

Brian Cahill, former Executive Director of San Francisco Catholic Charities, knows John's work with Samaritan House and with San Mateo youth east of El Camino. "But it seems his first love is the guys in San Quentin." Brian thinks they ought to give John a house on prison grounds to cut down his travel time. He is there on Sundays for Mass and also in the Protestant Chapel and to visit with the inmates. He is there Tuesday night with Vic and Brian for the spirituality group. He is there Thursday for the Restorative Justice group. And especially he is there and has been there for Kairos since it began.

Brian says that John is in no way naive about the records of some of the guys but he can see and respect the work they have done, the insight and remorse they have shown, and the spiritual journey they are on. And "no one is more affirming, less judgmental and more supportive than John." He is constantly pointing out to them that in many ways they are more evolved souls than some people on the outside. And Brian knows John's commitment doesn't stop if a man is released. He has stayed in touch with a large number of the guys who have been fortunate enough to get out.

Jeanne Elliott, Principal of Bayside Middle School, talks about John's long-time local involvement. She says that John Kelly has been a part of the Elliott family for years and that he was always extremely active in the Halfway House movement which is a rotating family shelter program among mid-Peninsula churches. John and Jeanne's father were actively involved in setting up the Halfway House in San Mateo and educating community members on the importance of reintegrating those who had served time in jail or prison. She says that "forgiveness and humanity was the theme of that work and this has been emblematic in all of John Kelly's efforts. He accepts us for who we are and helps us do good deeds without giving us a hard time about our failings."

Recently Red Moroney joined a seventeen member team that conducted a quasi Kairos weekend for fifty-eight San Mateo County Jail inmates. The prisoners really benefited and they are hoping that it will blossom into a more regular event.

Red says John Kelly and **Don Zamacona,** an avid Kairos participant who is with the Service League in Redwood City, organized this event through the correctional department. Red has done Kairos with John at San Quentin and John wanted to do a similar local program. They started with San Mateo Service League **Director Mike Nevin** (R.I.P.) to put the idea before **Sheriff Greg Munks**. After several months they got it okayed and put together a team of seventeen outsiders. They thought they might get twenty or twenty-five inmates but got sixty-eight. They were short outside manpower but it worked out.

On a Saturday morning (August 18, 2012), the group went in and some of the outside team members gave talks. They had discussion groups at tables of six inmates and one or two team members at each table. It was basically a Christian program with stress on personal growth and changing your life. Jerry Forbes served on this same San Mateo County Maguire Jail team and said they went into the jail and met inmates who looked at them and asked, "What are you outsiders doing in here? What is in it for you? Because nobody has ever done anything for me without wanting something from me." There was a palpable lack of trust.

The idea was to bring this to the County level as a kind of restorative justice concept. The basic principle is to get people to look at their lives and try to make some changes. Although the outside people give talks, most of the program is devoted to trying to elicit from the prisoners what's going on in their lives. What changes do they think they can make to better their lives both in jail and when they get out? The team spent two days there from 8:00 a.m. to 4:30 p.m. on Saturday and Sunday.

The response was "just fantastic." These people are really looking for something. Jerry says, "Now mind you, you get the cream of the crop in this program but it is kind of astonishing how many wonderful people are in jail." They screwed up in one respect or another but the point is to try to get them to achieve more insight as to what got them there and how they can avoid coming back. John Kelly points out that some of the greatest people in Kairos are lifers in San Quentin who really want to change their lives from within even though some are never going to get out. They become wonderful role models for the younger prisoners who are not in for such serious crimes and who are going to get back out. These graduates really do "a wonderful job of mentoring these younger people who can improve their lives and stay out of prison."

Red said he doesn't know that any prisoner had a miraculous change at the Maguire Jail program. But they seemed so appreciative that anybody cared about them. They couldn't believe that these people from the outside were coming in to talk to them to try to improve their situation and get them to take a look at their lives and how they can better them.

"It was one fellow's birthday so we sang happy birthday to him. He was almost in tears because he said he never had a birthday that he could remember." He said he was grateful that "you people would take the time to come and spend time with us prisoners."

They do a lot of singing during these programs. The prisoners sing the songs and by the end they think they are the "greatest thing going. It is unbelievable what the singing can do." They just all seemed "very grateful that we would do this and hoped that we could do other programs like this." Some of them really talked like they were getting in touch with Christ. They wanted to change the way they were treating people. One guy said, "I think this will help me to look at my fellow inmates differently; I really want to improve my relationships with the people here."

Jerry Forbes said the principles of the workshop are Christian but "it is not a preaching exercise." He says the difference in the men, the positive change in attitude over two days, is "almost indescribable." Jerry says the team went back for a three hour reunion and out of the fifty-eight guys, thirty-five came back. Some of the others may have been released since County Jail sentences are shorter than for those in state prison.

One of their outside team members spent six years in San Quentin. He gave one of the talks. He was at Red's table for one day and at one point he asked him, "Do you have any children?" Red said he had four. "What do they do?" Red said his son was a lawyer. "See, that's my point. I had a father who was a murderer and spent most of his adult life in prison. And my grandfather committed a homicide and spent a lot of his time in prison. And here I come along. I made up my mind – at some point I had an epiphany. Do I want my kids growing up and ending up in jail?" Red didn't know what he did to get prison but it was something that cost him six years. He said he came out, made up his mind to change his life and that his kids were not going to end up in jail. He told Red that he had five boys and the next day he was taking one of his boys over to start college at University of California, Merced. Red said it was a powerful talk and it really resonated with those other inmates. He had "been there and wasn't some old guy outsider like me."

Red started around 2008 and has done four Kairos. He hasn't done one in a year and a half because his wife became ill and is since deceased. She had a long battle with cancer and Red was her chief caretaker. John is getting him back into it and Red is also interested in doing some prisoner mentoring work. He says that is somewhat like a big brother type of thing for parolees. When they come out "there is nothing for them; there is no job; no programs, really." Red wanted to "do something to give back for all that had been given to me."

Ten

Sam Vaughn Success Story

I had the opportunity to interview an ex-convict who is and has been a friend of John's for many years. He is out, now reintegrating into society. Sam is a tall man who speaks and acts with confidence and energy.

Sam now works in the San Francisco East Bay with troubled youth and tells what it is like to get these kids to change when they are in this violent atmosphere. Sam made a profound statement in a John Kelly-sponsored speech to the San Mateo Rotary. He said that as they try to convince these kids to stay in school, the kids' answer is, "Why bother? I'll be dead before I'm twenty".

*Here is the story of **Sam Vaughn** in his own words:*

I was raised in the Richmond, California area. I work for the **City of Richmond Office of Neighborhood Safety** and we specialize in abating gun violence from a non-law enforcement standpoint – non-suppression – kind of like social work. We identify the folks we work with. We help those who are causing most of the conflict in the City. Though we identify, we engage them, work with them, mentor them one-on-one. Then we supply resources, helping them for substance abuse or to get their GED, their driver's license, documentation like Social Security cards so they can function like folks in society. Once they are to a place where we feel comfortable we try to find them employment; a lot of the times it is subsidized so they can get their foot in the door. The hope is, once somebody sees them working they'll be impressed and try to keep them on, unsubsidized.

"We've gotten a few success stories; sometimes not so successful because a lot of folks want something different but they don't know how. And even with guidance as far as family life, street code kind of gets in their way. But we keep focusing on them. In all honesty success is not just keeping these guys from pulling the trigger. We want more. We want them to be functional, happy citizens; which means a safer Richmond for all. I do this work because I am passionate about it. And I am passionate about it because I was one of the problems in the community. What that means today is that I've lived the same life that most of these folks live. I dropped out of school; sadly, I was able to just drop out of school. Getting in fights, getting incarcerated – there was no (social) net to catch me through that process. There was always discipline but nobody to look into, what is the problem; can we help this young man?

Tom Huening

"I was from a nuclear family; both parents working. I have two older sisters. We didn't have a lot but we didn't need for anything. We ate, we had school clothes and things of that nature. When I was about eleven my parents split and I never understood why until I was grown. But there was drug addiction; holding grudges against one another for things done in the past. So one day when I woke up in the morning for school my mom wasn't there. And so she stayed gone. And then she'd get into relationships which were kind of hard for me to understand.

"I did really well but I'd see both my parents hurting. Both my sisters were older. I was eleven and they were like thirteen and sixteen. They were kind of messed up – you know high school is tough for everyone. But no one got pregnant at fifteen. So my life went from being a normal household – identified with the Cosbys – you talk about your problems. You deal with them, sometimes not the best way. But it wasn't like the issues we were up against after the separation. So I really had nothing to pull on to deal with the problems in a positive way, in a way to help me become who I wanted to be.

"I was an honor roll student until the eighth grade: A's and sometimes B's and I tried to continue to do that. When the split came my sisters took my mother's side so I stayed with my father. I cleaned house, did his laundry, cooked dinner when he came home from work and was still getting A's and B's. I was just trying to get some kind of happiness around the household. I'm sure my father appreciated it but it wasn't enough – he was like, 'my life sucks.' So he was in the 'me' phase and just went bad. Both parents got really addicted to drugs; law enforcement issues, domestic issues. They started doing the things a lot of folks had seen their whole life but I had never been exposed to. So it was all new to me and very destructive. So I started doing what I saw. I stopped going to school because I wasn't getting any money; it was for drugs and alcohol. I wasn't getting school clothes. So then the embarrassment and humiliation came. So now I'm not going to go to school wearing the same clothes either with holes in them or too small. So I did what a lot of the young men around this community do: start providing for themselves by any means necessary.

"So I started selling weed. I started selling crack cocaine. Then I was getting things taken from me because I was new to the trade and kids had never seen me growing up so it was, 'Who are you?' So now I have to have a pistol so folks don't take what I'm working so hard to get. It was just a progression – a snowball effect. I ended up being right smack dab in the lifestyle that these young men that we work with are in right now. I didn't like it. The spirit within me was in turmoil. There was no peace in my heart or in my mind. And that just made it worse for me. And then I just gave up. Right after my sixteenth birthday I attempted suicide.

"So now I was dealing with psychologists and homes. By law they have to give you a seventy-two hour evaluation when something like that happens. And once again I'm a young man and I don't want to be here and my parents didn't know how to do what was best for me. They were into just making me happy. So they got me out of the home and I didn't get the treatment I needed to get. So I was still unstable. But at that moment I knew I needed to do something different. So I went back to school in the ninth grade. But then I asked myself, 'Why am I trying so hard?' So I just stopped. My third year in the tenth grade – I'm not going to be nineteen/twenty when I graduate. So I just dropped out. But I can't just not have an education, because then I can't get a job. The good thing is that I did have a positive foundation because of my first ten/eleven years. My father got up for work every single day; worked overtime. He made sure he gave me a good work ethic. I had seen that from a young age.

"I knew I couldn't get a job without a GED or without any skills. So I took the initiative and went to Job Corps. Nobody forced me. It wasn't court ordered. I figured it would be good for me to get away and do something positive. I got a GED instantly. I didn't have to go to school. They just gave me a test so I wound up graduating earlier than if I had stayed in school. And then I got a skill as a heavy equipment operator. So on my eighteenth birthday I was finished with Job Corps, and they take me to the union. I joined the union and came home waiting for work.

"I came home right back to poverty and despair. It wasn't like I was going to a new environment. I saw old friends and old bad habits and needed money. I'm now a grown man. It is not like I can ask for money here or there. So I've got to come up with something. I didn't even have money to buy drugs to sell, to have the start up costs for that. So I attempted a robbery and in the process I wound up shooting myself. Now I'm in the hospital for about three weeks and when I got out of there I said that I have to do something different.

"I wound up getting a job in a warehouse for about three months waiting for the heavy equipment job. I saved my money; ended up buying a car for transportation to the construction job out in Livermore. That worked out; ended up getting a union job, doing apprenticeship union work at like eleven dollars per hour. I was doing good and then winter comes. Now there is no work. So I worked maybe three and a half months that year and I'm not getting unemployment benefits because I've not put anything into it yet.

"So before I went broke I bought some drugs and started selling drugs to get money in my pocket. I ended up getting into it with someone over a bad drug deal and they claimed we robbed him. Now I'm in jail. I'm trying to do everything I can to get right. And I'm a young man and I'm using young-man's logic, so I was playing victim here; don't get me wrong. The good thing is I had this little bit of work history. Here it is about April and work is about to start picking up and I'm sitting in jail. My employer wrote a letter saying he definitely had a job for me so my attorney got me out on house arrest instead of doing a year in county jail. It cost about $100 per week for house arrest and I'm bringing home from work about $350 a week; plus transportation costs back and forth. I really don't have any money but I'm making it.

"The only place I had for house arrest was my sister's house and it's a crack house. They're selling crack. My sister is living with her boyfriend and his brother. The brother in law is selling crack and the boyfriend is selling methamphetamine. I asked them to please just have your customers meet you around the corner. I know you have to make a living. I know this is not my place where I can have my own space and can lock the door. I don't want to bring heat on you all and have you blame me. Because they (Parole/Probation/ the Police) are going to come; they have the right to come in here whenever they want to. But they just wouldn't stop selling drugs.

"So I know what I'm going to jail for anyway; so I might as well have some money in my pocket so I went right back to selling drugs. Then it became very profitable. I was getting good at it as in making a profit, building up a great clientele. They had just cracked down on Ephedrine to make methamphetamine so it was drought – now drugs were hard to come by so prices skyrocketed. I had a supplier I had known for years who could still get drugs at will. And I had folks who I was supplying and was making a lot of good money. But once you are doing well folks know and you have to protect yourself and once again I'm carrying a pistol. It is a mind set. I wound up doing that for years. I got my own place. I got two cars. I was nineteen years old. I was flying off to Cabo San Lucas; New Orleans for Mardi Gras; New York for the Fourth of July. I'm loving life.

"Right after my twenty-first birthday with no law enforcement activity I had just a couple of situations with some individuals that luckily didn't explode into loss of life. So after years and years of the dog-eat-dog mind set we're having a good time. We stopped at a convenience store for some nachos. I saw a couple fighting and thought it was humorous. The guy transferred his physical aggression to me. I was insecure and after having taken a couple sucker punches went out looking for him and found and confronted him. He had a weapon which I grabbed from him and hit him in the head with it. He wound up on life support and almost died. After some time I turned myself in and went to trial and was found guilty of attempted manslaughter which had a sentence of eleven and a half years with 85% which meant I would serve ten years. I was twenty-two and I've got nine years yet to do.

"They sent me to Corcoran Prison in Kern County. It is about a four hour drive from the SF Bay area between Fresno and Bakersfield. It was a miserable place. I spent two years there just doing time; reading, watching movies, playing dominoes, playing cards and going to chapel. For some strange reason when you get to a place where you feel there is no control you look to God. I definitely became spiritual – no I became religious – going to chapel every Saturday thinking God would forgive me and protect me in this chaos that I'm in. And He'll reward me because I'm doing what he wants me to do: going to church and reading the Bible; staying away from conflict. So it really wasn't a change in mind set – just a change in actions.

"I spent two years there trying desperately to get someplace closer to home and finally got sent to San Quentin in May of 2001. When I got to San Quentin it blew my mind. I was used to the only thing happening was church service for two hours on Saturday. That's it. Everybody got services once a week. No folks coming in.

"When I got to San Quentin I saw all these free people (outside volunteers) and all the activities and programs they had. These outsiders came in just because they wanted to help you be a better person. And that blew my mind. You know the stigma: at this time I'm a felon; I'm a convict; I'm in prison; nobody trusts me; everybody thinks I'm a scumbag. I don't really deserve to have them trust me. I haven't earned it. I showed them I am a person who doesn't deserve trust. That was just my mind frame and that's why I got religion: I've got God and God is never going to turn His back on me.

"Until I got to San Quentin I never worried about going to school. There were all kinds of folks I worked with in the construction field who were felons. All you need is a strong back and some common sense and a skill. I figured I'd just go back to construction and never worried about going back to school. I would just do my time and do it safely. But when I got to San Quentin they had a college program and I thought I'd be committing another crime not to go to college. Free college – can't hurt. Plus it's getting me out of the cell and homework is keeping me busy and making my days go by quicker. It didn't hurt that there were a lot of young ladies from Berkeley and Hayward and Davis coming in and teaching courses. It doesn't hurt to have eye candy while you are learning.

"I never really took up a lot of the self help programs about who you are, and what you need to be better, what you need to be emotionally healthy. I was just doing church and doing it at a level way more than just Sunday. So you could be an usher; they had Bible study; they had chapel every night with something going on. So when I wasn't in school I was in chapel and that was my life.

"And that's how I met John Kelly. Most folks would go to Protestant Chapel or the Catholic Chapel. John was a volunteer coming in and going to both. And that was interesting: those conversations with John about the differences between the two religions. I was learning about the history of how those religions came about, which was intriguing. John was always open and accessible and just had the persona that he was available. We talked about baseball and the things he had done in his life as a priest and now not being a priest. I was like, good for you; strong enough to make up your mind about what you truly believed.

"And that's why he bounced back and forth. He had a serious belief in Catholicism and what it stood for but had some issues with it. And he had some beliefs about the freedom of the Protestant Chapel to worship and he had serious issues with that. So he kind of intertwined what it took for him to be spiritual and fulfilled and just made it for himself. And that takes a strong person. It takes a very strong person to do that. And whether I agreed with some of the things he said or not, I just loved him for being able to have that strength and security to be able to say, 'I'm going to do what I think God wants me to do and I think I am intelligent enough to figure that out on my own. I don't need somebody to tell me.' And I just loved that about him. I looked up to him as a role model.

"So over the years we had a great relationship. Sometimes I'd see him there on a Tuesday night and go to Bible study in the Catholic Chapel. He encouraged me to take Kairos. And I think that honestly is when I began having a relationship with God – instead of just being religious and feeling like I was just doing a structure to please God. John helped me grow in a lot of ways. I was in San Quentin for six and a half years and he was there the whole time. The longer I was there the more days of the week I would see him. And he just really became a role model. And as hard as that seems for some folks to understand, since at that time he was early to mid seventies, he was able to engage nineteen and twenty year old gang bangers. Norteños, Sureños, black folks from the East Bay. The way you could just engage with him; to look at him as a friend. He never really had the persona of mentor. He always came as an equal which attracted people to him. But he ended up being a mentor to everyone anyway.

"He just amazes me. We really, really got along well in there. He helped me mature as a man and grow in my spirituality; but also in my mind frame. He encouraged me to get involved in stuff other than just church because he understands how that can control you. And if something happens that may break that relationship in any way, like if the pastor of your church who you look up to, is sleeping with somebody, so now you question everything you believe in. He said there is more out there for your spirit than just the chapel. That's where the self help comes in because they're talking about your spiritual and emotional well being and just not using God or Jesus in the wording, but it is the same concept. And things can go wrong and you can still be well. So that was a definite nugget that I needed. So I got involved in those other things. And our friendship just continued to blossom.

"When I left prison I didn't leave John. He actually performed my wedding in February of 2011. It was a renewal of vows since we never had a proper wedding. So he definitely is a part of my life, though I've been real busy so I don't get to hang with him the way I would want. I've seen him a couple of times since his health problem. I'm glad he is getting back around. But that walker is just killing him. I don't care what anybody says about him – he is a proud man. He hates having to be taken care of. He hates having to depend on people. And I know although he hates walking around with that walker, what he would hate worse is not being able to get anywhere. So he's able to be like, this is better than the alternative – not as good as it could be but it's better than the alternative. And that's like his persona and what he promotes. His life is like take the blows the way they come and hope your integrity and character can get you through it the best way possible.

"John hasn't lost his ability to speak and that's his gift from God; his mind and his ability to express what it is he feels and to encourage folks like me. I don't think God would take that from him: 'You ain't goin' to walk but I'm not going to take that. This is your work on this planet for Me.' And I really believe that and I think he believes that too. And John is a ham. He doesn't even need a microphone, he talks loud enough. He loves to share his God given gift. He loves singing also. In a group you can hear John above everybody else. He needs that. He has never experienced a lot of the things in life that everybody else has experienced. He has never experienced his own family and has never experienced that attention that you would get. I think in some ways that might just be John getting what he needs. Every human being needs that attention. I laugh at it, 'Why do you keep doing that? But keep doin' it because we love you to death.' And it doesn't bother me.

"John is innately good. He is positive in the spirit of God. It dwells in him on a regular, regular basis. Most of us, it is more times than not that we try to make our own peace. And I don't know about when he was younger; he might have been fumbling and doing all kinds of stuff at a younger age. But ever since I have known him I recognized that he is driven by the spirit, more times than not, which is not true for most people.

Tom Huening

"I went to the San Mateo Rotary and spoke. It was very interesting and spoke once again to who he is; to make that group of all elder, Caucasian individuals even be interested in restorative justice. That shows the trust they have in him. He's not that guy who everybody is looking at saying, 'Look at this dude hanging out with them folk.' He also has that very professional and eclectic group of folks that he deals with on a whole other level. From what I saw he receives their respect and admiration just across the board. That is a feat in itself; hard to juggle. But you can't fake it. Everybody identifies just who you are and John is just his person, his character, just who he is. What you see is what you get.

"I think another thing that attracts people to John is his lack of interest in material things. John doesn't have an income. I don't know that he got anything from the Catholic Church. And everything he receives now is like a gift. It is as if folks still view him a priest and they just follow the word and take care of those who are spiritually blessing you. So he had folks who were paying his phone bill and those who pay his car insurance; somebody who would gift the rent for his apartment. So everything that he had was because somebody wanted him to have it. So he is literally like a monk living in poverty except folks wouldn't allow him to just live in poverty. But he doesn't ask for things. He doesn't go and see a watch he'd like and give a talk and charge $500 so he could get that watch. He just wasn't that person. To live in this world in this day and age in this country with capitalism at its finest, to be like John is rare – rare like a white unicorn – didn't know they existed.

"To put one word to it: he's amazing. Very few people in this world have a legacy to leave. Once they are gone, pretty much it's over. The folks you have everyday dealings with miss you the most but even those move on and get beyond it. They'll remember you on your birthday. There are very few people in this world who you can say their name and people would recognize it and he is definitely that person. You say his name and you will be hard pressed to find somebody who doesn't know something about him. So I think this biography is a great idea so that folks who may not have ever met him can still know him and know what he represented. I am grateful to be part of it."

Eleven

Reforming Criminal Justice

There is no political issue more important to John Kelly than the current state of criminal justice and how our society treats criminals today. John sees the lock 'em up and throw away the key approach as un-Christian and a foolish waste of redeemable human talent. John is especially critical of the California Parole system that seems more focused on retribution than public safety.

John points out: "In 1980, California had twelve prisons and 20,000 inmates. Up until about 2010 we had thirty-three prisons and 170,000 inmates." The only reason the number has since decreased is that California has farmed some prisoners out to private jails in other parts of the country and the State is now sending prisoners back to the counties. Whether a prisoner is held for retribution or rehabilitation matters a great deal.

The recidivism rate of those who are incarcerated has been "in the area of seventy percent over the last umpteen years." That means that nearly everybody who gets out is back in prison within three to five years. And John points out, "Obviously something isn't working." (Many are returned to prison for technical violations; see: http://www.urban.org/UploadedPDF/CA_parole_exp.pdf)

John worries about the lobbying power of the prison guards union. He says there are some really great prison guards but "their whole union doesn't want things to change. That union is just as powerful as the school teacher union; maybe even more so. A report three or four years ago said that there are four thousand prison guards in California making over $100,000 per year because of overtime. So if things change they wouldn't get that much money. That is a driving force whether we like it or not."

"We've got to have prison leadership and staff capable of determining whether a prisoner would be a danger to society or if instead they've reached the point of rehab where they could be a plus to society." And this evaluation cannot be based solely on whether or not they strictly followed prison regulations. John calls it a tragedy that in our prison system, a guy makes one rules mistake and that becomes his permanent label. The prisons demand more perfection than others do on the outside. "There is a lot involved, I admit. Their conduct over the years, they all get written up for different things (breaking prison rules)." But incentive needs to be reestablished because now with determinate (fixed-term) sentencing, good behavior counts for nothing.

A prisoner about to be released will have sent many signals about whether he'll make it on the outside or will return to crime. John says, "It's just by how they have been conducting their lives inside prison. Have they really been committed to helping other people inside? What kind of programs were they involved in? Did they become better educated? Did they take advantage of training to be effective when they get outside?"

John says lifers are unique in terms of recidivism. They have been locked up for twenty or twenty-five or more years and they have either vegetated or (mostly) they've wised up and changed. California Department of Corrections did a study of lifers who were paroled between 1990 and 2010. "There were 988 who were paroled and only thirteen reoffended and none of them for serious crimes."

(Similarly, for the time period 1995 to 2010, 860 murderers were paroled and only five returned to jail or prison for new felonies – none for life-term crimes. However, "A lifer's prospect of actually being granted parole by the Board of Parole Hearings and not having the decision reversed by the governor is – and always has been – slim." From 1991 to 2010 that probably has ranged between zero and seven percent. (blogs.law.stanford.edu 2011)

John says many of the folks in prison have changed their lives – they are redeemed people. "I certainly feel for their victims and their families, but society has not accepted that forgiveness is possible and important." There hasn't been a willingness to accept that criminals can reform and be an asset to their families and society. "I've met some genuine and caring men in prison. They have completely changed their outlooks and lives. Not all, of course, but we need a better system of evaluating prisoners for parole and release back into society."

John doesn't believe all inmates will change. He came home from San Quentin on a recent Sunday aware that the whites of San Quentin were currently locked up and kept in their cells because some of them picked on a sex predator and "beat the holy hell out of him." The way the prison administration processes these issues is that something happens and they lock up everybody of that race and then analyze it.

This shook John up and he wondered what the thinking was of the guys who did the beating and what the end result was for the guy who got beat up. What chance does a sexual predator have of changing? "Do we respect the fact that they are also human beings? Is there some way we can assist them to change what they need to change? It seems to me that the general tone is that sexual predators are almost impossible to change. Is there any experience with ways that you can change those people?"

John says of course that's also how people feel about murderers. It is generally thought that they can't change so lock them up. John comes home after meeting with the nine Kid C.A.T. guys and some in his outside group will ask if he is crazy because he respects them now as human beings even though they did "this horrible thing." John hopes that people are beginning to become aware that the guys in blue (the prisoners) were themselves victims. "It is difficult to understand what horrors some of these guys went through growing up trying to survive. One of the guys in my meeting group said he had nine different 'fathers.' His mother was all over the place. He had no stability whatsoever growing up. Some of the stepfathers beat him up. By the time he was fifteen years old he'd gone through pure unadulterated hell."

John heard an inmate say that growing up in that kind of atmosphere you develop a mountain of rage inside. And you don't know what to do with it particularly when it is happening to you as a young little kid with no power. How do you get it out of your system? Who's there to help you? So this guy said at the end of his Kairos weekend that he looked at himself and realized he had all this anger. And he said, "What I have been doing up till now is using it to hurt people. The problem is I ended up hurting myself more than anybody else so I think that's not the way to go." When John shares these inmate stories with people who've led a relatively normal life they can't understand what it is like to grow up this way. They can't appreciate the real torment some of these prisoners have had to survive. And yet many are able, with help, to rehabilitate themselves.

Restoring Justice

John says, "Criminal Justice, as we now have it – somebody commits an offense and the whole purpose of how the State deals with it is: How serious is it? How much time do we have to give the offender? And who cares?" And John adds that if there are victims, their only purpose is to determine the seriousness of the offense and to know what happened to them so the State knows what to do with sentencing.

John notes that there is a huge difference between defendants who can afford a private lawyer and those who get a court appointed defense lawyer; and that there is a huge difference between how different courts handle things in San Mateo, San Francisco, and the Bay Area compared to the east side of the state. There, he says, "Forget it – the defendant gets clobbered. It is a whole different ball game." What can we do to ensure more equal defense representation?

The basic concept of restorative justice is that "something goes wrong: a breakdown in relationships among people. It is a breakdown in how the community should function." To deal with this breakdown "the entity should be directed to two key things: healing and restoration." In the current criminal justice system "that's not much of a priority."

The nearly unique thing about San Quentin within the thirty-three prison California justice system, it does have rehabilitation. John attends a graduation ceremony every year and the fellow running the education program said that there are about three thousand people who come into San Quentin every month to help people. John has a thirteen page list of the kind of self help programs that go on inside San Quentin and John plays a regular and substantial role.

John describes his current week at San Quentin: "Tuesday night we have a group called Spirituality. Sixteen inmates and four outsiders discuss, How can I change my life? Or, How do I find some peace in my life? Past topics have been How to deal with anger, Empathy, and How to forgive." John wishes he could record some of the comments made by the inmates (not allowed) as the discussion goes around the table. And these inmates come back every Tuesday night.

After a recent Thursday noon speech to the San Mateo Rotary John travelled the nearly forty miles to San Quentin for a session on Restorative Justice. This group has been ongoing for seven years and John has been there from the beginning. On this particular night there were seventy guys in blue discussing elements of restorative justice. They were taking responsibility for "what I did; being aware of all the people I hurt; finding some way that I can possibly make their life better; being aware of all the victims that were in my life." They asked what they can do to change the atmosphere in our communities so this doesn't keep happening.

"Our prisons and local jail systems are not very geared to restoration," John puts it mildly. John is on the governing Board of the San Mateo County Service League so he has been involved in the local County jail. John calls the recent local jail retreat a "breakthrough." Prisoners there are now feeling good about themselves; they are sharing good thoughts with each other. They are "gung ho." The team went in a couple of months after the retreat as a follow up and saw new looks on their faces and new energy. Hearing about that exercise, the woman who runs the women's jail asked that a retreat be put on for the women.

John's point is that if we can start developing the mentality that restoring is something we can do, "our primary energy around people who end up incarcerated will be to help them immediately get well. We can help them change how their life is going." San Mateo County is building a new jail and John is sitting on a planning committee to ensure the new facility has "enough space to have programs to help people change." In the next few years more and more inmates will be coming back locally from State prisons and "we could have people hanging around our jails for as long as five or ten years." John asks, "Do we want them to sit there and do nothing or do we want to get them to change?"

In the federally mandated shift of State prisoners to local jails "money is important, but how do we protect public safety? If we have these guys sitting there doing absolutely nothing we can only expect them to come out and do the same stupid stuff all over again. Healing and restoration are what are important."

John also argues that "this society has a long way to go in dealing with the needs of victims." He observes that those who have been offended by someone committing a crime have substantial amounts of fear, anger and frustration and asks, how do these victims recover and get healthy? John attended a seminar on restorative justice attended by a young lady whose house had been invaded. She was totally shaken by the experience, afraid to live in her own house and afraid to do the things she normally did at home. She said all the criminal justice system wanted out of her was, "What happened, and how can I help convict this guy?" It seemed that no one cared what happened to her.

The State of California is "horrible in the way it treats victims." They do not take into consideration the needs or trauma of the victims or their need for rehabilitation. John notes that the Victims' Rights Office of the State of California is in the same building in Sacramento as the Department of Corrections and Rehabilitation. John does not think that is an accident.

John is particularly troubled by the Board of Parole Hearings system and its effect on victims. "There are times when the Board doesn't want to make a decision." In these cases they have an En Banc Hearing where people can testify before the whole Board in favor of or against an inmate. John has sat through three or four of these hearings and the tragedy is to see somebody who was a victim, now twenty-five years after the crime was committed, "spouting out venom against the criminals. They actually have helped destroy their own life in the process." There is a "desperate need to find a way to really help the victims."

Inmates are also victims. An example is the first person who talked at the recent County jail weekend retreat. He is a friend of John's who spent time at San Quentin and now is doing "fabulous stuff in the community". His early-life story blew John "out of the water." When he was born his father was in prison and his mother was a drug addict. How does he survive? And how do we break this cycle?

How do we develop in our own community an atmosphere "where we can reduce the possibility of crime so it doesn't keep happening?" One thing we can do is what the San Mateo Rotary club does – reach out to disadvantaged kids and let them know that somebody appreciates them. "The club aims at all kinds of people in other cultures around the County giving them a chance to succeed. They have awarded many scholarships to young people over the years."

John cautions that, "There are all kinds of people in our country's criminal justice system whom I do not want to see out on the streets. No question about that. And we have those kinds of people in our local jail system as well. But please accept the fact that people can change. Please accept that I will testify that some of the people I have met through the years at San Quentin, not only have changed themselves but are some of the most effective people in helping other people, particularly young people, change.

"An interesting thing about San Quentin and even the County jail is that these guys realize that a straight and OK adult can pay attention to them and think they are OK." And once some of these guys change they commit to help their fellow inmates change. In San Quentin there are long term lifers who have changed their lives and who run most of the programs.

Most lifers put in substantial time. Of John's friends who have gotten out over the last few years most served twenty to twenty-five years and one served thirty-two years. Some have spent more time in prison than they have spent outside. Part of restorative justice is to help released prisoners reconnect with their communities and their own families. Sometimes, though, their family was the problem in the first place. So it is important to find out before a prisoner is released if they can go back to their family and reconnect. Will they be returning to a family that is going to be supportive?

It can be a big challenge to keep functional families together. If you commit a crime in San Diego you may be sent to San Quentin in northern California. How much family connection do you keep while there? A lot of prisoners get out and have to start over with a brand new support network.

To help prisoners when they get out, one goal of restorative justice is to create more transitional housing. There is a place in Oakland called Options where a lot of guys have been going. They have to reside there for a period of time and are given a chance to reacquaint with the community. "There is a desperate need for more of this to happen because these men are left out to dry in a lot of ways. A question for many communities including San Mateo County: Is it willing to develop facilities for the released prisoners to come and spend some transition time? The Service League does have five and six unit places in Redwood City that provide a transition for women. We need more and more of that kind of thing."

Student Lecture

John talks to many groups and I had an opportunity to interview John in front of San Francisco State University students interested in communications and criminal justice. This was a natural environment for John the teacher and supporter of youth. John believes that youth will be the agent of change needed to reduce crime in our communities. The classes were "Leadership Communication" taught by **Jennifer Kammeyer** *joined by* **Dr. Karen Lovaas'** *class, "The Rhetoric of Criminality and Punishment." The lecture recapitulates and summarizes John's view on restorative justice.*

John began by bragging about his Serra High School teaching claims to fame: S.F. Giants' **Barry Bonds** was a Serra student but John claims no connection; New England Patriots' quarterback **Tom Brady** was baptized by John; and John performed Football Hall of Famer Lynn Swann's first wedding.

John led off with the statement that "one of the major disasters in the last twenty or thirty years in California has been the criminal justice system." He went on to describe the fix as a move to Restorative Justice which he defined as "Number One, the Offender: What did he do? Whom did he hurt? Number Two, How do we take care of Victims whose lives get disrupted in a major way? And, Number Three, How do we change our communities so all this horrible stuff doesn't keep happening?"

John challenged the students to imagine if the California Department of Corrections and Rehabilitations changed its focus: the minute somebody is caught in a crime the authorities start figuring out how to make that person well, not only how much time they will have to spend locked up to make sure they do not disrupt the community.

An inmate must first take full responsibility for what he did and for the number of people he hurt. Then he must decide what he can possibly do, not only to take care of himself, but how he can take care of others. "The lifers tend to be way ahead of the short termers when it comes to change. Many are thoroughly committed to find a way to impact the outside world and make sure that kids don't end up doing what they did."

John realizes that inmates have done some "pretty horrible things." But he is also aware of the "unbelievable ability of human beings to change." In a year-long Victims and Offenders Education program every inmate is challenged to clearly understand what he did and thoroughly understand the people he hurt – not only the victims but his own family and community. The inmates write a letter to their victims that doesn't necessarily get sent. The point is that the offender writes about his awareness of the seriousness of what he did.

Alternatives to Violence is an exceptional Solano State Prison certification program John described which trains about forty inmates to counsel other inmates. When visiting James Alexander *(his story is in the next chapter)*, John was amazed at how other inmates would smile, say hello and thank James for all he had done for them. When John first met Alexander at a Kairos weekend in 1995 he was very shy and afraid to get up and talk in front of others. Now he is out of prison, is extremely active and is frequently invited to participate in this program. "It does happen, people can change."

John told the students about San Jose journalist **John Hubner** who wrote the book *Last Chance in Texas*. Hubner watched the rehabilitation process in the Giddings State School, home to "the worst of the worst" juveniles incarcerated in Texas. Every kid had to write the story of his life. Other kids then acted out all the characters in the kid's story in front of him. If the inmate kid could not understand the depth of what he did and show some empathy, he was so far gone that he could not be rehabilitated.

John told the students about a young man recently released from the old San Mateo County Maguire jail. He hadn't before committed a crime but happened to be going around with some guys he shouldn't have. These guys invaded a house, took some stuff and this guy was the driver. He was convicted and spent six months in the County jail "absolutely doing nothing, just sitting there; a total waste of time. We should have restorative justice to rehab these people and have some way to change their thinking without necessarily even having to put them in prison or jail to do it. It's possible; it can happen."

John gave another example of a guy from his group in San Quentin. He got out on parole, found a lady friend with a little boy and they lived out in the country on a farm. His parole officer came by and found the boy's BB gun and "violated him for breaking parole." The guy went back to San Quentin, sat in a place called West Block for six months doing absolutely nothing. They finally let him out. But for him "it was another total waste of time and energy."

John described how beginning in the mid-1970s and up to the present time, the tough-on-crime movement has built up more and more. The State of California passed "some of the most insane initiatives" to make it increasingly difficult for people accused of crime. Then Governor Jerry Brown did "a very disastrous thing: in 1976 he changed the criminal sentencing process from indeterminate to determinate." Before that, if someone was in prison with an indeterminate sentence he could reform and get out sooner than otherwise. Jerry Brown's determinate sentencing acted to fix an end date. As a result a lot of inmates decided that they were not going to work very hard at reforming themselves because they were stuck in prison until their fixed end date, so why bother. That made a huge difference. This change and initiatives like Three Strikes and others, according to John, "are absolutely insane."

John knows no "lifer" (prison sentence of 10/15/20/25 years to life) who has served only his minimum time and most are not released until three, four or ten years later. The Kid C.A.T. prisoners sentenced as teenagers are now in their early thirties and have spent more time in jail than they have spent outside.

At some point, John explained, a lifer has the opportunity to appeal to the Board of Parole Hearings to find out if he is suitable to be released. John thinks less than ten percent of inmates even get a hearing. He says three Board of Parole members go to a prison to interview an inmate and decide if they are suitable for release; their recommendation goes to the whole Board for a final decision. The Board of Parole Hearings is a Governor-appointed body and as long as John has been involved "everybody on the Board has had a criminal justice background – even though the State says the Board composition should be a mixed group across California society."

John told the students that in 1988 the State of California passed statewide ballot Proposition 89 which provides that even after the Board of Parole Hearings gives an approval, the governor has thirty days to decide if he wants to accept their decision. **Governor Pete Wilson** was "horrible," approving something like five percent; **Governor Gray Davis** was "absolutely abominable -- he said, 'I will never let a lifer out while I am governor.'" (From 1999 to 2003 he reviewed 371 parole grants and only approved nine.) **Governor Schwarzenegger** approved about thirty percent, but the current **Governor Jerry Brown** "has been fantastic" and is now at "eighty-five to ninety percent approval." (For detailed governor release data see: Crime Victims Action Alliance: http://www.cvactionalliance.com/)

John told the group that he had attended the En Banc hearing of James Alexander in Sacramento where fourteen or fifteen citizens testified that James "was one of the finest human beings they have ever met. But a District Attorney's office representative from San Diego came up and shot the whole thing down, and James was turned down." James finally went to court and the court decided that the Board had treated him unjustly. "The excuse that the Board uses over and over again is the severity of the crime."

John told the classes that he got a letter once from someone who wrote that their son-in-law had been murdered on the street in Palo Alto by a gang of Tongans who are all now in San Quentin. The writer asked since John was in there would he look them up and tell them we are not angry with them and that they should simply change and get well. John saved that letter and considers it one of the most powerful letters he has ever received. "I think that is courage." John relayed that he has never seen anything more moving than to see an offender and a victim sharing together what they have both experienced in trying to reach restoration. "It does happen."

Another San Quentin program he described was Malachi Dads to help inmates become better dads and how best to play the role of a parent. For many guys the big tragedy of their lives is that they have not been able to be the parents that they ought to be.

John finished the student lecture by reciting the pledge that the inmates recite every Thursday evening at their session at San Quentin, the Restorative Justice Pledge:

- I believe that violence is not a solution to any problem
- I believe that every person is endowed with a sacred dignity
- I believe that every person is capable of changing, healing and being restored
- I pledge to respect the dignity of every person
- I pledge to overcome violence with love and compassion
- I pledge to accompany and support anyone affected by crime on their healing journey
- I pledge to be an instrument of restoration, of forgiveness and reconciliation.

Twelve

James Alexander Success Story

I met James (Alex) in a coffee shop in Santa Rosa, California. To look at his neatly pressed shirt, sharp slacks and clean shave you would not have guessed James Alexander was an ex-con. I found him articulate, intelligent, friendly and confident.

James Alexander told me he met John Kelly in October of 1995. He said, "John came in as part of the Kairos Program, the three day Christian based workshop. It is extraordinary because there is a group of prisoners who are meeting these (mostly white) guys who come in from free society. From the get-go, we are treated as though we are human beings, not prisoners. They look past the prison blue uniform and they see souls. I was struck immediately because John Kelly is a tall figure and has that deep voice. He commands attention just by his presence. I was fortunate enough to be at John's table in San Quentin prison. So we talked and I was impressed immediately, not just by his presence but by his sincerity. We connected immediately. After that weekend I continued to be part of Kairos inside. When they would have other weekends I would volunteer to serve. I became a part of the Kairos family at San Quentin.

"But something happened, say six or seven months later. I ran into a bit of difficulty inside the prison. I began to question my faith; I had pretty much given up on the church because of an incident that happened at the church. It was not related to Kairos but to one of the fellow Christians at the church, we had a bit of a disagreement. I did not know how to resolve it so I stayed away. John Kelly, having not seen me around, inquired about me. I wasn't going around the church and also not going around any of the other places in the prison. I was kind of isolating myself. I was becoming a bit of a loner. So this one rainy day I was walking around the lower yard of San Quentin prison, called the recreation yard, a huge recreation yard at the bottom of San Quentin. There were not too many inmates out because of the rain; it was really coming down and everybody's inside. But I'm out walking around the circular track in the rain, pretty much alone. I had been sentenced to a life term in prison. I didn't think many people cared about me. I had pretty much given up after twelve years.

"So as I'm walking around that track in the rain, I see these two figures in the distance, one tall and the other shorter. So I wonder why these guys are out walking in the rain. As I got closer I recognized the taller guy and it was John

Kelly. I asked, what are you doing out here? And he says, 'Looking for you.' He says, 'Alex, where have you been?' I was just blown away by the fact that he would come down and look for me. So we talked and it helped me get past my feelings of depression. He helped me get back into the Church. It helped me to reclaim some of the relationships I had walked away from – some of the people who had had an interest in me. He kind of saved my life. I hope that doesn't sound too over dramatic. I might have been one of the .... Who knows? I don't want to even think about it.

"He helped me so much. He said he wanted me to get involved in other programs too. They have a Toastmasters speaking program here. He said, 'Do it.' I said, I'm so shy. I can't get in front of people. I hear my Chicago accent and think, what is this guy talking about? 'No, go for it.' And I did. I got involved in the Toastmasters program. And that first speech, I was in front of twenty or thirty people, and I was trying to give this little speech. I've got buckets of perspiration coming off my head but I got through it and I survived. And I kept going and I got better as time went on. As a matter of fact they made me president of the club about a year later. That's the kind of effect John Kelly had on me. Had he not suggested that I could do it, get involved, I would not even have thought about it. He believed in me and that is huge; that is huge.

"I think that is a feeling every man should experience. I think most men experience that from their fathers ... but when they find someone.... My father passed away in 1984 when I had just started my life sentence. Anyway, John believed in me from the beginning; from my first meeting at that Kairos table from our discussions, I knew. That is huge. When you have somebody who believes in you, you can do anything.

"I grew up in Chicago, born and raised on the south side in the Village Project. My mother remarried to a security guard and we moved further west out of the projects when I was eleven years old. There was a lot of alcoholism with my stepfather and subsequently my mother; it was difficult. But I was in school and still doing well, so much so that I got selected to go to Lane Tech High School, the best public high school in Chicago at the time. It took me about an hour to get there in the morning. I had to take two buses. I was doing well academically but I still didn't have that many friendships. Lane was a predominantly Caucasian school; the number of blacks that went there was actually quite limited. So I didn't get invited to too many parties. But I wasn't too sociable anyway because I had a weight problem; I was overweight which forced my self esteem down.

"When I was sixteen I was kind of smart as a youngster so I was helping people out with their school work – the guys on the football team. This one guy named Gary, he was a big football star and I had helped him a lot. He was one of the most popular guys at this big high school. Gary was having this party at his house and it was the event of all events. I'm in the hall at school and Gary is walking by with all his buddies and he stopped and said, 'James, I want you to come to my party.' I was like, whoa, sure, I'll be there. So the whole day I'm thinking I'm going to this big party. So I get back to the house and I told my mom. She asked, where was it at? Over on the north side. She asked how I was getting there. I'm taking the bus to get over there. She asked what time the party started. About seven or so. She says no you're not going way over there. Aw mom, this is the biggest party. I'm sixteen; I want to go. She wasn't having any of it. So the night of the party I waited until they had a few drinks and they kind of forgot about me and I snuck out. I took this bus to the El (Elevated) train and then all the way to Gary's house. I got over there and there was real loud music and they had kegs of beer. People were throwing up. And nobody was talking to me. So after a few hours I couldn't put up with any more of it so I just left.

"I remember taking the bus back to the El and thinking, what a waste of time. I should have listened to my mother and stayed home. It's never as good as you think it's going to be. But what can you tell a sixteen year old who's looking for acceptance? So I got on the El and took it to Lake Street and I guess it was Pulaski. I get off the El and I'm on the platform walking toward the end and there were some guys there who wanted some money. And I didn't have any money. Because I'm overweight I guess I looked older. And I had on a leather coat. My father had given me a leather coat for my sixteenth birthday. My father had been out of our lives from when I was three years old until I was about eleven. He had been absent from our lives. When he came back it was off and on – 'I'll do what I can.' My mother had already remarried but it was my real father who gave me this coat. They wanted to take the coat from me and I didn't want to give the coat up. So we struggled and even though I was overweight I was kind of stocky and it was a tough struggle; they had a hard time. I felt a knife going in my side and that's all I really remember. Evidently I was thrown off the El platform and landed on the ground below. Luckily it was snowing and I landed in the snow. But I'm told I didn't get found until five o'clock the next morning. I had lain out in the snow all that time.

"Then in the hospital I had been pronounced dead on arrival. Maybe somebody saw when I came in and thought this guy might be better off dead. I was told that a nurse saw me on a gurney and if she hadn't responded to me who knows what would have happened. She said, 'This guy is still alive.' So they rushed me into surgery and sewed me up. My clavicle bone was broken and I was just a mess. I was paralyzed from the neck down and didn't have any movement in my lower extremities or my arms. They wanted to cut off my foot but I begged my mother not to let them cut my foot off. They came to me every day and would stick me with these needles but I felt nothing. And a lady would come in every day and change my bandages – take the old ones off and put on a new set. But I couldn't feel anything.

"One day the doctor comes in and sticks me and, 'Oh, I think I felt something.' And he sticks me again and he runs out and my room fills up with these guys in white coats. 'He's getting his feeling back.' And sure enough, the nurse who changed my bandages came in and ripped my bandages off and I felt the worst pain I ever felt in my life. I was thinking if they ever made any human being who enjoys dispensing torture it must be this lady right here. I cried out so loud they must have heard me throughout the entire hospital. I was so glad for all the times I couldn't feel it. But maybe that had some effect in bringing me back to health; who knows?

"So after about three weeks of trying to get well they allowed me to go stay with my father. My mother thought it would be best for me while I rehabilitated and learned how to walk again. It didn't work out too well because he was a bachelor at the time. Having an overgrown sixteen year old in the house at the time kind of takes away from the lifestyle he was used to. So after a couple of months I said I had better go back home to mama. Eventually I was able to walk with crutches. I went back to the southwest side. Summer had passed and my mother said I had missed so much time at school – from December all the way through the school year. So they said I'm going to have to repeat the year. I told my mother I can't repeat a year. The only thing I had to hold on to, my little self esteem, was education. I said I wouldn't do it. There had to be another way. My mother did some checking and they said the only way you can stay in your grade was to change schools and go to the neighborhood high school. So that was the compromise and that's what we did.

"The neighborhood high school was Manley High School. The outside of the school looked like a war zone and the inside was worse, just terrible. The books that they were reading from were old raggedy books and they were books that I had read two years earlier at Lane Tech. I thought, there is no learning going on here. I told my mother that I could teach the class. The teachers there were just trying to survive. My mother said well, you have to finish so you get your diploma but it was just a tremendous waste of time. So I put up with it. There were fights going on. And I spoke a little differently than some of the kids there and that automatically made me a target.

"So it was not going well and I get the bright idea – I'm seventeen (my birthday is September 13, I'll be 50 years old) – that hey, I'll go join the

Marine Corps. I'll go into the service; anything to get out of that school. So with a buddy of mine we went down to the office of the military recruiter. The recruiter had his uniform all nice and sharp. We go in and he talks to us and I'm sold and I'm ready to sign the papers. So me and my buddy are filling out these forms. Back then they called this program the 'Buddy System.' He looks at my buddy's form and says it's fine. He looks at my form and says I made a mistake right where it says age; you have to be eighteen to come into the Marines. 'You put seventeen so you have to fix that.' So I tell my buddy, 'I'm not going to do this,' and he says, 'It's OK.' So we step outside and he says, 'Listen, don't you want to come in with me? The man is telling you to just put down eighteen and we are done, we can go in.' So we went back in and the recruiter asked, 'So are you eighteen?' And I said, 'Is there any other way this could be done?' He said, 'Well you'd have to get your parents' permission. You want to do all that?' So I said, 'Yeah, I think I had better do that.' 'Then I can't get you in today.'

"So my buddy is all mad at me and I go to mom's house. I'll never forget my mother and her sister are in the kitchen talking and laughing away. I said to my mom that I had something I wanted to talk to her about. 'Mama, I want to go in the Marine Corps.' They both burst out laughing – a loud laugh. 'You have got to be kidding; you came out of the hospital a few months ago, you can barely walk. You can't go into no service like that. There is a lot of physical activity.' I said, 'I can do it.' Then everything got serious. I said, 'I have no life; I have to try to do something – to live. And this is it; this is what I want to do.' She says, 'Well, think about it tonight and we'll talk about it in the morning.'

"But nothing changed. I woke up the next morning and found my mother at the kitchen table and told her, 'I want to go.' She did not want to do it but she signed the papers. It must have been 1979. March of 1980 is when I went in. *(James exhibits some sad feeling and I ask what's that about.)* I think that was a big change in my life. My whole life kind of changed right there. My mother really didn't want to sign and I kind of forced that.

"I went into the Marine Corps. I did relatively well. I went in at 185 pounds and three months later I came out 135 pounds. They worked my butt off. They tried to get me to drop out from the beginning. I still wasn't physically fit, having just relearned to walk. Some time had passed since I had signed up and I was committed. I had been running every morning before it was time for me to actually go into the Marine Corps. I was doing as much as I could to try and get myself in shape. They did everything they could to get me to drop out. But it was my last chance, my last hope; there was no way I was going to drop out. When I first got there one of the drill instructors called me a chocolate Pillsbury Dough Boy. And he ate on me. Any little thing he'd come up with, he'd make me do extra – push-ups, exercises. I didn't do anything wrong but they stayed on me. Well, maybe in hindsight it worked. But it reminded me of having my bandages removed – torture. At the graduation ceremony the same drill instructor said, 'Won't your mother be proud of you.' He turned out to be a good guy.

"My first duty station was Camp Foster in Okinawa. I was also TAD (temporary additional duty) in Japan for a while. We were in WESTPAC (U.S. Navy Western Pacific) and also went to the Philippines for maybe forty-five days, and also Thailand and Korea. I did get the humanitarian service ribbon. Everybody on the ship got it because we picked up some of the Vietnamese refugee boat people. I was in communications as a radio operator. I was away for about a year. It seemed like a lonely existence. Came back Stateside and found out I was going to be stationed at Camp Pendleton, California; and my older brother was stationed there. He was also in the Marine Corps. He and his wife lived there off base. Her brother also was a Marine who lived off base with his girlfriend.

"So I didn't know too many people when I got there but I thought I would make friends. Unbeknownst to me my brother's wife's brother was about to get kicked out of the Marine Corps for dealing drugs. But over the course of a few months he befriended me. He had these yard parties and I'd go over but I was kind of naïve to what was going on. I was just happy that someone wanted to be my friend.

"Months later I get a knock on the door, I just finished my shift, got out of the shower, went to the door and it was him: my brother's brother-in-law. He said he needed my help on a drug deal gone bad. So I agreed to go with him and his friends to a drug dealer's apartment and nothing good came of it. I was the youngest guy, the shortest guy and the guy that they gave the gun to. I didn't know it at the time but the weapon had a hair trigger. So when I went into the apartment I lifted the weapon up and it discharged and so in March of 1983 I took a man's life.

"I went through a lengthy San Diego jury trial with three women in the jury who saw my young twenty year old self sitting up there. They thought that I shouldn't be convicted of the penalty; that I should get a lesser penalty. They just had so much sympathy. But it was three of them and the other nine guys on the jury said that he did wrong and he's got to pay. They were really on these women to try to get them to change. But the women didn't give in; they stood up to those guys. I guess one of the women whom my attorney spoke to after said that 'it was a mess – all the drugs and all those people dealing drugs – they are hurting each other.'

"People testified on my behalf. My first sergeant testified on my behalf; my commanding officer. So I had some great guys talking up for me. But the women didn't give in and they told the judge that they couldn't reach a decision. So the judge told them to go back in and try some more; they did but came back and said nothing had changed. So he ordered a mistrial. My real father had told me on the telephone, 'The most you can hope for is that they come to you and offer a plea bargain so they can avoid another trial and not have to go through that.' And sure enough, the District Attorney came with a plea bargain for manslaughter. The lawyer that I had been given, he was a public defender. He advised against me taking a plea bargain. He said we put on a good case the first time. He said he could do it again and maybe I could go back to the Marine Corps. There should be a law against being naïve. At the time manslaughter was serious time. So I said OK, we'll go through another trial. So as I was being escorted out of the room, I swear I could hear him tell the District Attorney that by going through this second trial, the lawyer would be able to buy himself another car.

"So the District Attorney said we were going to go through another trial. But before I started the second trial my father passed away of a heart attack; 39 years old. I've carried around a lot of guilt for years about that. The second trial, there were not too many women on the jury, definitely not three. They didn't convict me of first degree murder. I was scared to death of that. But they convicted me of second degree murder which was a fifteen years to life sentence at the time. So I went to Soledad Prison. I had never been in prison before and it was pretty terrible. I couldn't sleep so a guy gave me some pills that were supposed to help you sleep. I had them on top of my little shelf. I had been taking them and they did help me sleep. An officer came through in a routine inspection, saw the pills there on my little desk top and says, 'This is a violation.' So he wrote me up for that. So I couldn't have those anymore. It was just a terrible experience.

"I ended up getting into altercations and got sent to San Quentin for the first time in 1986, to teach me a lesson. They put me in the worst place in the worst part of that prison that they can put you in. They put me in isolation hold, as they call it. It was about eighty percent death row inmates and twenty percent regular inmates. I met some characters in there. **Charles Manson** was in the tier below me. We had a lot of gang members in that section; guys who were the leaders of like the Crips Gang. I met all these people but I was trying to survive which was difficult. Because every time we went to that yard someone would get hurt. Then the administration would have their perfunctory investigation which always lasted ten days. Always ten days. So someone would get stabbed today, we'd be locked down for ten days and on the tenth day they'd let us all back to the yard. This would play itself out again and again and again.

"And there was shooting out there because they had the gun towers. And the gunmen, their guns would always be trained right there on the yard. My first time on the yard, I had a scruffy beard because I had been in the hold when I got shipped to San Quentin. So you know, scruffy beard, they strip search you and wand you with a wand to make sure you don't have any metal on you. So I saw this other inmate over here with clippers cutting other inmates hair. I thought that looks good so I go over to him, 'Can you knock this off my face?' He said, 'No problem, I'll get to you.' And sure enough he did. So I stood up and I was dusting the hair off and I hear a shot. You are immediately supposed to get down on the ground. So I got down on the ground. Sure enough, the guy who had just cut my hair stabbed a guy. He tried to throw his little inmate manufactured weapon away in the little gutter but there is no way you can throw anything away there. So the officers came by, put handcuffs on him and led him away. Other people came by and put the victim on the gurney and took him out. Then they stripped search all of us right out there on the yard. Then put the handcuffs on us and led us back to our cells. And so this is the routine that I came to find out. And that happens repeatedly. When I got back up to my cell I got down on my knees and said, 'Oh God, where am I at.' I'm 21, 22 years old.

"So anyway, I prayed and prayed and prayed. So after this I had to make a decision whether I would go back to that yard. *(Did you grow up with religion?)* My mother put us into the Catholic school but we really didn't go to the school; we weren't really 'on the books' meaning we were not registered. But there was this one nun who took a particular interest in me, perhaps because I had a speech impediment as a little guy. I couldn't pronounce certain letters that started with an S or a Q or a C. I can remember sitting there on her lap and she'd be trying to get me to pronounce these words. I was just a little kid but I can remember thinking, 'God she had a long nose.' I had to look right at her face and her tongue as she said the words. I don't remember her name but this lady was a saint. We're talking forty-five years ago but she helped me so much. I look back at that part of my life as the impetus to get me on track educationally. It was for only maybe a year. And that spirituality stayed in me. I wasn't a regular attendee at church but I never lost that connection; that part of the Creator is in all of us. I knew he was in me. So I've had that all through my life.

"So trying to decide if I would go back into the yard, there are two things that could happen. You could get labeled as what they call protective custody where the guards protect you. They take you off the yard and put you with other prisoners who need protection. So I could do that or go back to the yard. That was my choice. So I don't want to go to the yard and get killed. But then again, I'm doing a fifteen years-to-life sentence. I can't be isolated away all that time in protective custody. (He did make the decision to go back to the yard.)

"I was in prison for twenty-eight years from March of 1983 to April of 2011 and parole technically for life, but unofficially after five years you could be released.

"The Kairos family in San Quentin, whom I met through John, we were able to stay in touch. Even when I got shipped off to Old Folsom in 2001, John Kelly found me. He is always finding me. *(big smile)* In 2001 he came up to Old Folsom and found me. I was in the midst of depression. I had been doing so well at San Quentin; I worked in the x-ray department and got my technician license. So I x-rayed the general population and death row inmates.

"I maintained a friendship with John and he would actually write support letters for my parole hearings. John's letters were very well written. But even after his letters the parole commission still said no. But one of our Kairos outside brothers who was in the Kairos weekend in October 1995 was **Eugene Kirkham**. He and his wife **Cody** would come and visit in Old Folsom, I think around 2002. They were getting to know me. So they asked the question, 'Why aren't you getting out?' So in 2004 Eugene got his California Bar license renewed – he had earlier gone into the wine business. He went to Harvard and Boalt Hall in Berkley. In 2006 for my parole hearing he was going to be my attorney. (The Board signed off and found Alex suitable for parole but the governor said no. In 2007 the Board again found him suitable but Governor Schwarzenegger again said no. Same story in 2008, when there was a three year minimum before returning for another hearing.)

"But John Kelly with our support system kept involved; you could say he was the glue that held together our Kairos family. After the 2008 turn down I wanted to give up but John Kelly and **Pat Tubman** and her husband (Pat was also one of the helpers of the Kairos team) said that you have to find something; you can't just give up. I didn't know if I could do three more years. I was in so much pain that I didn't know what to do with myself. So I went into a California Coast University College correspondence course with some encouragement from John. That gave me some focus and when I got my first A in my first course I thought I can do this. Pat Tubman and her husband were putting up this money and some of the other supporters were helping to pay for the legal costs. I said if she and her husband were paying the money I can do no less than the best I can do. I thought if I can get an A on the first course then I can get an A on the next one and I did.

"I started staying up until one o'clock in the morning because it was too noisy to study during the day. So I went to the restroom inside the prison and used the light there to do the work. There were guys coming in doing all sorts of nefarious stuff, things we don't want to talk about. They said, 'What is this guy doing here with pen and paper?' They'd think I'm taking notes or something. And so I got another A and kept getting A's. And when I finally got out in 2011, in January of 2012 they conferred on me the Bachelor of Science degree in Psychology – summa cum laude.

"John Kelly and some of my other supporters went to Sacramento to speak on my behalf in 2009-2010 in front of the full Parole Board. That was a disappointment because I couldn't be there. But it didn't turn out well, not at all. The governor would not relent. So I came up again in early 2011. I went to the Board and again they found me suitable for parole. We were all set to wait for the five month process to validate the finding and get back to the new Governor, Jerry Brown. But after a month or two we never made it to the governor. It was because the same California Court of Appeals which two years prior had denied the San Diego Superior Courts 2008 order that I be released, upheld a second order that I be released. So on April 13 of 2011, I was released.

"So I got out and **Gene**, with his wife **Katrina** and former wife Cody, were waiting for me here in Santa Rosa. The three of them were waiting for me and I had on these old sweat clothes. They took me to a nice restaurant in Calistoga where I ate halibut which I had dreamed about. They said, come to work for us at the winery; we'll find something for you to do.

"This coming Tuesday at 10 a.m., I will be interviewed by Sonoma County Alcohol and Drugs Services to be an alcohol and drug service counselor. I have my California Association of Alcohol and Drug Abuse Counselors license. I've done the written examination and I need a certain number of counseling hours to get the license. I have the credentials and the degree and out of seventy-three applicants my standing was sixth." *(James (Alex) has secured "on call" alcohol and drug counseling in St. Helena and is working extra-help with Sonoma County. He has written his autobiography and is looking for a publisher.)*

"John Kelly is the number one reason that I am sitting here today. If it hadn't been for the impact John Kelly had on my life, I wouldn't be talking to you today. This man has assisted me far beyond what is called for. We've got this personal relationship. I mean he's helped me like I was his son. He's been there for me. I talk to him once a week. I am so grateful to him and glad to have his presence in my life, his spirit in my life. He is a great father to have – Father Kelly."

Thirteen

Thoughts on Religions

John evolved from sincere seminarian to successful Samaritan helping folks like James Alexander. Living the roles of parish priest and high school teacher he learned the "official Church understanding" of Jesus. All Catholic literature and liturgy are reflected in who the Church proclaims Jesus to be.

But John could not reconcile that doctrinal image with Christian activity in the real world. For John's subsequent thirty-three non-priest years he has re-looked at who Jesus was to him. John today describes Jesus as a "god person, thoroughly evolved as a human being, thoroughly God oriented."

San Mateo County Supervisor **Don Horsley** once asked John if he believed in God, and "he said that he did." Don asked about Jesus. John said that he believed "that when the world got too screwed up, God sends someone like Jesus, or Krishna or Mohammad."

John explored Eastern spirituality. "If Jesus is so obviously *the* son of God and the *only* one who brought truth into the world, why hasn't he caught on in other parts of the world? What is going on in those other areas to replace what we believe Jesus is?" In Eastern spirituality John learned about arriving at liberation and self awareness. He was exposed to the "full knowledge of what it means to be a human being and to be connected with the God force totally in every phase and moment of your existence." John believes "that's what Jesus ended up becoming – or perhaps he was already there when he was born."

John uncovered other spiritual choices. He notes that "other people in history, other cultures have discovered this same God force." One book John studies nearly as much as the Gospels is the *Commentary on the Bhagavad Gita*. Another is *How to Know God* which is "based on the full understanding of all eight steps of Yoga, not just the exercises." John says the lessons are the same: "every human being walking the face of the earth has the potential to become self-realized and has the *responsibility* to become self-realized." Many prophets, gurus or avatars have brought us understanding about how we go about doing that.

John says Jesus came into his historical culture to bring people awareness in that particular time and place and, if they could grasp it, to spread it to other times and places. But that spiritual awareness has also happened in other places in the world. In January 2002 John went to India for a Yoga experience with the Himalayan Institute that professes the belief that the eight steps of Yoga will bring people liberation.

John was introduced to the Himalayan Institute by the guru Swami Rama (who touts the ability of any person to achieve peace without the need for a structured religion) and his book describing the full understanding of Yoga and the various steps to get to liberation. John subscribed to their magazine *Yoga International* which he finds "profoundly spiritual and realistic." In late 2001 the magazine advertised a pilgrimage to India called the Maha Kumbha Mela which takes place every twelve years based upon a certain alignment of the planets and stars. Considered a time of healing, people gather in the city of Allahabad in the middle of rural India. This spiritual celebration attracts about forty million people over a couple of months.

John's group left out of San Francisco, flew to Hong Kong, Singapore, then New Delhi. The New Delhi airport was filled with homeless people sleeping on the floor and "it was just sort of a mess." They took a ten hour train ride to Allahabad passing a series of little country towns. John remembers the little sign that warned not to use the commodes in the stations since they emptied right onto the tracks. John saw signs advertising Coke and Pepsi but also one in English asking if you were having problems with sex and if so to contact counselors. "Their culture was totally different from ours."

They stayed at a Himalayan Institute property developed as a retreat center and walked to a little village nearby. John realized the cute little kids they saw would probably not go more than a couple hundred yards from where they were born until the day they died. There was "not much culture going on" for them. But they were happy, delightful kids.

John and a couple of hundred Westerners attending this institute pilgrimage stayed in tents overlooking the Ganges River. In-house celebrations were held and occasionally they'd walk down to the Ganges and join the larger celebration. John was fascinated. At the in-house sessions a number of Indian gurus talked about their lives and their hope to have India reach a balance between Eastern spirituality and Western technology: "that our cultures would help each other out."

Once the Dalai Lama came to visit in a big tent meeting area where John was no more than five or ten yards away when he walked by. They had all removed their shoes out of respect and when they came out "everybody scrambled for their shoes but for some reason somebody took my shoes and I had no shoes." John had to take a taxi three or four miles to his camp and luckily had a spare pair of shoes.

In their free time they took a boat ride into the central area and John remembers passing a dead body in the water. January twenty-fourth was the main day of celebration and the big thing was a dip in the Ganges. "I did get out of the boat into and out of the water fast. All I know is that when I came home all the skin on the bottom of my feet peeled off slowly but surely."

John concluded that Eastern understanding of Western spirituality was that "we are ritual oriented and not focused on dealing with concrete issues like justice." And John's understanding of India was that "they have this great history of spirituality but through the caste system they have separated humanity into sections and it is pretty hard to cross over." John fears that as India grows in technology and Western awareness it will affect very few people and "that the poor are not going to get anything out of it." John thinks India's economic growth has been confined to thin little sections of the country and the rest of the country "is primitive as hell as far as living conditions."

The saddest and most frustrating thing John witnessed was on a two hour bus ride to the spiritual town of Varanasi. Going through small towns "on one side of the bus you'd see all these kids dressed to the nines going to school – a lot of the schools are run by the Christian missionaries. Around the other side of the bus sitting by the roadside were the untouchable kids in rags who weren't allowed to go to school. That whole untouchable thing is horrible to see in action."

John reflected that listening to their gurus was like hearing Bible stories. He concluded that the seminar message was "exactly the same message as what Jesus said." Since Jesus had no multi-media and there was then little communication among parts of the world, John concluded that "this God force brought his message to different parts of the world in different formats and in different structures."

John now considers Holy Scriptures, including the Bible, as the teaching of morality under the guise of reality. The stories are not literally what happened; rather the message is supposed to come through the story. John said that Jesus spoke in parables as the best way to convey his message.

John currently goes to Sunday Mass at San Quentin "to be with his buddies." But during the ceremony he redoes the wording of the liturgy in his head "because it doesn't fit with who I am." "The language of the Mass is so archaic, non-growth oriented and not oriented to present reality. It had a purpose if you think of Jesus with his buddies at the last supper. But whatever he wanted that to be, unfortunately isn't what it is anymore."

According to John's reading of the gospels, Jesus had a horrible time getting anyone to understand who he was. "Sure he created a lot of energy and excitement but there were not many people who really grasped what he was about. When Jesus saw what had been going on in his day and saw that it didn't work, he started making people think differently."

Tom Huening

That Jesus died for our sins makes no sense to John "as if there were a God who demanded redeeming." John says that Jesus was a political rabble rouser and the religious and political leaders could not stand to have him around. He was a "shit disturber and they had to get rid of him because their power base was being overthrown."

I agree that Jesus was a rabble rouser. The story of his act of disrupting the money changers in the temple might have been the final straw to the politico/religious leadership who knew then he had to go. It seems to me that Jesus as a Jew was not interested in starting a new religion but only reforming the commonly known abuses of Judaism.

John is fascinated by the apostles. "Even at the Last Supper when Jesus is about ready to leave and trying to set up his heritage they are arguing about who is the greatest among them; about which of them is going to have the power. They totally didn't get what he was all about." And John appreciates the story of the rich young man who kept all the rules thinking he was wonderful. But Jesus told him to get rid of all that junk – "give your belongings away and give your life to people." *(One look at John's old, beat-up Honda Civic convinces you that John subscribes to the principal of minimum materiality.)*

John notes that there are a couple of things in the four gospels that people really don't pay attention to. Almost every day of the three years that Jesus was out there trying to educate the populace, behind the crowds were men called Scribes and Pharisees. John says that these "hecklers continuously tried to screw him up and to show that he didn't know what he was talking about. Jesus went through hell and had to retreat to solitude every day to put himself back together based on all the crap he had to endure."

One of the tragedies, and "why I could not be a priest anymore is that Church liturgy is all window dressing and looking good. It is having people singing and getting all excited and then going home and forgetting everything. They see Jesus as a mythological figure, not a real person."

John believes that the God who put this universe together built potential for growth and development and trusted human beings to make it happen. But we have gotten waylaid. "One of the sneaky ways we cop out is to say that Jesus is *it*, once and for all, and nothing is ever going to change." He says, "That's what fundamentalists are all about, but it's a cop out – that means we don't have to do anything but sit here and bask in something that happened two thousand years ago."

"The Catholic Church is stuck in a lot of those kinds of ruts." The Church is now going back to earlier stiff, formal language in liturgy after having made a few small changes in the last ten or fifteen years. They say, go back to tradition. John says that some ministers in established religions use tradition, ritual and dogma or the original scriptural language as a power base. They have enough followers who don't want to think for themselves that they get away with it. So it all becomes fixed instead of being open to change.

John says that a big difference between traditional religion and progress in religion is that "traditional truth" is fixed once and for all; but actually it is a dynamic and progressing reality. "The God that I believe in put into this world the possibilities to continue to generate new and exciting things. Much organized religion has made a point of critiquing everything based on what Jesus said 2,000 years ago. But grains of truth from Jesus need to be reinterpreted as history plays out."

Disciples who interpreted Muhammad said that his was the last word. Bahaullah said the same for the Baha'is: no additional prophets for one thousand years. Some Buddhists claim there cannot be another Buddha until the words of the original pass away (like never). Are we seeing a pattern here? Rather, I agree with John's belief in progressive revelation.

We all know that Science has advanced enormously and helped humans to increase our knowledge of our world; but in religion not so much. Many if not most religions still adhere to the same beliefs from a thousand to three or more thousand years ago. And ironically, unlike fundamentalists today, the folks of those earlier times most likely understood their scripture stories as stories. They knew metaphor from literal fact.

John's nephew Patrick, with seventeen years of Catholic education, asks who is actually living the Catholic life today. He said that John challenges the traditional message and has reinterpreted his faith by asking how Christ lived and how Christ said to live.

John has thoughts about the Church Sacraments – what they really are supposed to be, and what is the purpose of ritual and liturgy.

The Eucharist: John says that when Jesus was coming to the end of his life, he knew "he was going to get clobbered and very aware it was about to happen." In John's gospel Jesus talks about all the things he stands for, all the things these apostles are supposed to do, their whole purpose; what's supposed to happen after he leaves. The food is a binding force, a celebration; as in family gatherings, food is a symbol of togetherness. So when Jesus said, "do this in memory of me," he meant on a regular basis get together and share a meal. Share how you are doing and your spiritual progress. "Suddenly we get a literal 'This is my body?' Really this is a symbol of Jesus being present with the apostles. But having the bread transubstantiate (The Catholic Church doctrine that the host actually physically changes into Jesus' body) – who cares?"

The Eucharist should be like a family meal. The language of Eucharist is so different from this. "One line in there that I will never say until the day I die is: Lord I am not worthy. Just before you are about to share the food you say: Lord I am not worthy? What does that mean?"

John thinks back at St. Mark's parish "it actually was people coming together to reinforce themselves as people to live a decent life." On Holy Thursday they had their community space set up as a banquet hall, they'd go through the liturgy and then have a meal. To John, that was the whole purpose. And they had the place jammed. To that degree "I was a renegade and I think I was a renegade in the right direction." And the rule that only Catholics at Mass can receive the Eucharist – "If somebody is there who feels in the spirit, why would I say, I'm sorry, I can't give you this?"

Protestants at San Quentin only have Eucharist the first Sunday of every month. Their caution is, "If you do not believe that you are saved because of Jesus Christ you have to question if you should participate. If there is something now in your life that keeps you from being connected you should consider refusing the bread." John shares the bread simply because the inmates are all his friends. He feels connected with them because of the Kairos weekends, because of the programs they have done. "And we are supporting each other. How many Masses do you go to where you get that feeling? We used to get it at Serra High School with the kids."

Baptism: For John Baptism was traditionally "about washing away original sin, our supposed moral congenital defect." Catholic schools still teach that you are starting out defective based on the horrible things that went wrong with Adam and Eve, and only because of the grace of God do you become healthy. John thinks God had made us correct to start with and gave us a chance to be healthy and whole. John does like the symbolism of life coming out of water. "Even Jesus talked about being reborn through water: he came out of the water committed to the fullness of life. If there is such a thing as original sin, it is the fact that there are two different karma strains in the world: good and evil. You are born into a world that has a certain amount of evil that you will be challenged by. Through Baptism I come out of this living water to commit myself to living and resisting evil."

Confirmation: John asks, how many cultures have a ritual around reaching adolescence? "This is a reaffirming of the commitment to make spirituality part of your life now that you are old enough to become aware of what life is all about and to gradually become independent." John thinks "it is beautiful if you do it right. Doing it wrong is somehow getting zapped by the spirit that makes another mark on your soul that makes you special."

Matrimony: When John performs weddings now as a Christian Minister and a Universal Life Minister, he says "you are marrying yourselves. I do not marry you – I celebrate your commitment to one another. It is only valid if you have worked hard enough before you have come to the ceremony that you know who you are, what you want to do and that you are really committed to sharing a life of love and growth." John asks four things of a couple: 1. Are you really communicating with each other? 2. How do you handle money? 3. How do you get along with your in-laws? 4. Do you or don't you want to have kids? And is that a mutual decision? John brought that question up to a couple and one said "I don't want kids" and the other said "Oh, yeah, I want kids." John said, "Wait a minute, this conversation ceases right now. Go home, sit down and figure out a mutual answer. If you get one then come back; otherwise, forget it."

John regrets that the Catholic Church decrees marriage as a sacrament and that it is definitely for life and if you do anything to split you are forever evil. "And thereafter you are condemned. Pfhuuett!" *(Not sure how to transcribe the sound John made)* Human nature being what it is: "There is no guarantee.... I do everything I can when I marry a couple to make sure I am convinced that they have the basics of life ready to go and they have indicated that they mean to stay together and be effective parents." John allows, however, that there is no guarantee that people are going to continue to grow together and share in this experience equally.

John thinks one of the worst things that happens in the Catholic Church is when couples stay together out of sheer fear and spend miserable lives together because they were never really in love and they never meant to share. During the last few years that John was a priest, when people had been divorced and wanted to re-marry he would find a Protestant minister and they would do the wedding together so the couple would know that John was "still on their side." He didn't want a married couple staying together five or ten years after they realized, hey, we just don't work as a couple. John tells couples that "their relationship is more important than just having kids" and that having kids is not an excuse for staying together. Kids cannot put it into words, but "kids know exactly what is going on."

Confession: "If a kid came in and didn't say he masturbated a few times and had dirty thoughts, I'd say to myself, What's wrong with you, kid? Are you unhealthy?" John studied psychology so he could be more effective at understanding what people were telling him in confession and help them figure out some practical, real ways they could change if they wanted to. "I could tell them to say five Our Fathers and five Holy Marys and bless them but they would be back in a week or two doing the same damn thing." The thing is to be able to sit down, "not necessarily in that cute little old box," and actually have a conversation based on: Where are you coming from? What's going on? What do you see you need to change? And help put it into a life process for them.

The San Quentin guys go through self help programs and start changing their thinking and their basis for making decisions. One of the best talks in Kairos is called Choices: going from reaction to response. John describes it as, "Instead of just reacting to whatever is going on, whatever you are feeling, sit down and ask, what is the long-term effect if I keep doing this? And start changing the way you make decisions." John says that if penance is going to be effective within the Church it should be a way for people to "internalize what's going on and how they become better instead of just rattling off a bunch of prayers."

On other Church issues, John is not opposed to men choosing to be celibate as part of their priesthood if they understand what sexuality is and know what they are doing. "But most of them don't. A lot of the people my age who remain priests, those of us who were in the seminary in the forties and fifties, were not taught about sexuality. Most of the sexual crap that happened recently in the Catholic Church happened with guys who were around my age."

And John asks why the Church worries about homosexuality. "Give it up! Why fight it? If God is a God of love and he is responsible for this creation and he does everything for a purpose and for good, why does He make ten percent of humanity have an inclination to be homosexual instead of heterosexual? I defy anybody to tell me that a homosexual sets out to be homosexual. Who in the world would do that? My point is that God either made a mistake and therefore He is not this wonderful Being that we say He is, or there is a reason. I'm sorry; it doesn't make any sense to me."

John also points to the Vatican trying to ding the U.S. Catholic nuns for being too liberal. "Well, the nuns are right on – their whole thing is about dealing with justice." John tells of an article by his San Quentin buddy Brian Cahill about Catholic bishops coming down on nuns for not following the rules. The Church is angry because "the nuns won't support the Church's ruling on abortion and sexuality and women being ministers." One line in the article is "exactly where I'm coming from: that is that the nuns are only interested in helping the poor and establishing justice."

John thinks nothing is worse than the power of "fuddy-duddy white priests" based on "pseudo spirituality." Still today John is uncomfortable when called "Father" by friends and former students. "That title is part of the power play and is brainwashing." Attaching and expressing that reverence to another ordinary human being seems only a way to maintain status and authority beyond the norm. Does another human being other than one's blood father deserve that title? It seems to imply that we are in the child role in relation to a priest.

John is not even convinced the early Church thought that Jesus Christ was the *only* Son of God. That concept later became necessary for Christianity to tell the world that "we are Number One and everybody else comes in second. If the Catholic Church doesn't change it is not going to survive." Christianity's survival depends on "having people come together to talk about what Buddha, Mohammad and what other spiritual leaders of the world had to say. How do we connect, not how do we fight." John believes that is starting to happen and that Jesus will fit into that scenario.

The Church has been "subject to Western and even Eastern influences and is now beginning to let women be real human beings when before they were servants or property." John as a priest used that passage from St. Paul that wives must be submissive to their husbands. "Where did that come from? Jesus associated with women in opposition to his culture. He had women buddies."

Doctor Bill Schwartz, the free-clinic champion, says he and John would talk philosophy at times. John, of course, is Catholic and Bill is Jewish. Bill says he has never had a religious conversation with another person like he had with John. Bill says they were different but never had the problem of "I'm right and you're wrong. It was mainly about how we can relate to others to make the world a better place. And we decided we are doing it. He's doing it from his religious path and I'm doing it from my religious path and both lead to the same place. Both Catholicism and Judaism have as a main tenet service to humanity."

John notes as the bread and wine are being prepared at Mass the text of the prayer is "…the fruit of the vine and the work of human hands." John thinks this symbolizes what our whole earthly role is. "On one hand earth and vine, God will give us what we need. Our job is to work to make it productive and ongoing until the world ends. We need to take what God has given us, discover it and use it for justice and good."

Conclusion

As author I've interjected *comments* here and there, but I'd like to wrap up with more detail about why I chose to write this John Kelly biography.

I began as a freshman student at Notre Dame High School in Niles, Illinois in 1956, the same year John began teaching at Serra High School in San Mateo, California. I was not a good student and was frequent trouble to the administration. I would have been a regular attendee at John's "jug" after school disciplinary sessions. Like John, I was a Catholic true believer and still holding the religious cards I had been dealt by family and Church community. Not until after college and military service and reaching age thirty did I realize that I had spiritual choices.

John as a priest had more at stake but I could relate a bit to his separation anxiety. I decided at a single Sunday Mass that I could no longer buy the rigid Church dogma and that I could no longer be a Catholic. I stepped into a religious vacuum for some thirty years until revisiting my own spirituality in the form of my book, *Spiritual Choices: Putting the HERE in Hereafter.* In a parallel fashion we realized we didn't need formal religion to be spiritual. I sense John and I each decided that how we *act* toward others was much more important than what we were told to *believe* in Church.

I don't have the same capacity to work with society's disadvantaged that John does. What I hope to do with this biography is support John by spreading word of his advocacy and helping advance his passion for compassion and restorative justice. I believe in John but I have no interest in canonizing him. My hope is only to leverage John's voice and expand the discussion about religious and especially criminal justice reform. John works on an organizational level but he is no policy wonk. He is mostly a one-on-one, hands-on kind of guy. His individual approach, though, forms the basis for some serious consideration of prison and parole reform.

Preventing social ills rather than trying to cure them has long been a guiding principle for enlightened social and government leaders. Yet the bulk of public budget money goes to cure: cure in the hospital; cure in the jail. Shouldn't we instead as a society allocate much of that same money to prevention? That's what John has in mind working with troubled youth and creating better conditions for all people in our communities. I think most would agree that with effective prevention we'd all be better off long term. But there are important special interests: law enforcement, judges, doctors, nurses, welfare workers – people whose jobs depend primarily on the curative approach as opposed to prevention. It is a challenge to make that shift of funds, but where the money goes is really where our goals are.

I've been involved in local government at a policy level for many years and believe the public sector Job One is maintaining and enhancing public safety. Stated simply, I believe dangerous criminals should be locked up to keep them from harming others. However, many politicians have played to the public's fears, sometimes sidestepping the simple truth that the great majority of prison and jail inmates will eventually rejoin their communities. If inmates have been merely warehoused, will we be safer when they get out?

There is a lot we don't know about criminal acts and the criminal mind. We know little about brain chemistry and the nature of evil. We do know good people sometimes come from horrible circumstances but that poor social conditions often produce poor social results. Inner city slums produce more crime than affluent suburbs. Is science now capable of predicting who will commit serious crime? Will it ever be?

A prime question for Americans and especially for Californians is why we have so many people in jail and prison. Can we bear that cost when the alternatives might be funding education or improving the broad general health of our neighborhoods? Are we safer having so many non-violent people locked up in prison?

These are not just questions for criminal justice experts and politicos. Ordinary citizens with good information and relevant choices come to reasonable and workable conclusions. John's case is not going to provide statistical analysis but he is showing us what success looks like, at least in a few important cases.

I'm no criminal justice expert but as a parent and grandparent I feel responsible to help make our social environment safer and better, even if just a little bit. Beyond telling John Kelly's story, I advocate taking a closer look at victimless crime, drug and alcohol and mental health policies and their *measured* effects. We need to review the California and U. S. parole policy and analyze the unintended effects of technical violations not associated with a new crime that put people back in jail, perhaps disrupting their family and job. Unnecessary incarceration is expensive and crowds out funding for other forms of public safety.

John Kelly is not about cost/benefit ratios and analytic studies. What he is about is demonstrating the good that comes from showing responsible adult attention to young potential teen gang members. He knows that even among people who have done wrong at least some are willing to change and become an asset to society. John works on helping inmates find their cure but he is helping them and us in the prevention of future criminal activity. John is mostly about helping one more person find the good in himself. Compassion and forgiveness are John's watchwords.

I once compared John to Jesus but that seems not exactly right. But think of the good works and social change Jesus brought to his world as a man rather than as God and the comparison feels better. I believe John has accepted the responsibility to make the best use of the gifts given to us generally and especially to him personally to do unto others as he would have them do unto him. Jesus seemed not so much about the outward prayer and devotion of his Jewish heritage as he was about actually physically helping the disadvantaged and downtrodden in his world. John does that in our world. John's joy comes from doing the meaningful work of helping others.

I have shared John's life lessons and have learned in the process. Following the daily-action life example of Jesus and many of the world's great spiritual leaders has served John and his community well.

While others pray, he provides.

Your comments are welcome at: JohnKellySamaritan.com

After Words

Personal Comments About John

Of all the people I interviewed, no one seemed closer and more in touch with John Kelly than his longtime friend, Pam Frisella, Mayor of Foster City. In lieu of her own chapter I've given her substantial space here where she adds a special element to the understanding of John as a person.

Pam Frisella: "John is unique and the most solely his own person of anybody I know. He is the closest to being Jesus-like – and I tell him this and he gets all embarrassed – because he saw the need to feed the hungry and clothe the poor." John has few worldly goods, "as we know from cleaning out his apartment after his stroke. Material things mean absolutely nothing to this man." She says that John has given the last five dollars out of his wallet but he doesn't give the money so people will go away; he gives the money and then stays until there is probably nothing more that he can do for that person.

It is the emotional part of John that Pam sees. "I mean he lives it, he walks the walk; he lives his beliefs." People think he is not religious anymore because he is not a Catholic priest but that can't be further from the truth because "Jesus is still his leader." She says he has done everything "the way that he sees Jesus wants him to do it. And he stays with it. People might help others once in a while, and then they'll go to the spa instead of giving a hundred dollars to the poor."

John has taken Pam to San Quentin and she has worked a couple of Kairos teams with him. He's opened up another part of Pam's life. She says "I would have never seen this except by talking to lifers who can be delightful human beings, who just because they made that one mistake in their life, now have to pay for it."

Each of the last four years Pam has had a birthday party for John. The event becomes a reunion for the parolees he has helped. As Mayor of Foster City, Pam told the police "not to run any plates" on the Saturday night of the party because the parolee guests were not here illegally. "This last November we had about forty people; they brought their spouses and a couple brought their kids. They worship John because he was their advocate. He never ever has given up on them."

Years ago Red Moroney Sr., Red Moroney, Janet Jones, Dolores Kelly-Hons and Pam had a little bit of a social group going with John as an active member. They would go dancing someplace in Foster City, California. Pam said that was a different side of John. She wishes that "he could have known a romantic love." When John was in assisted living in Burlingame recovering from his stroke he made a comment to Pam one day that "made me really, really sad." They had a little music group playing love songs and John was watching Pam and some obvious widows who were looking kind of melancholy. You could tell they were reliving memories, and John said that then he realized that he had never had a relationship. Pam thought it must have had to do with twenty-five years in the priesthood and after that maybe he had a fear of getting into a relationship. Pam remembers that there were a few women who were after him when he headed Samaritan House. *(She would not mention names.)* But he did not want to get involved with anybody in a romantic way.

Pam thinks John is becoming more aware of how he misses the personal connections from when he was a priest. "When he had Church services everyone came forward. The attention and help he got after his stroke in December, 2011 reminded him that attention feels pretty good. During his initial stroke recovery he'd say that there were just so many visitors that he didn't even answer the phone. But he would count how many people stopped in that day. Even though he sounded like he was annoyed he really wasn't." Then all of a sudden the attention had fallen off again, because people now think he is OK. People email Pam and ask how John is doing and she gives them his home number and says, "Why don't you call him?" She says, "That is the message we have to get out to people."

Patrick Kelly has known John all his life and maybe is his closest relative.
Patrick Kelly: "It has always been fun Uncle John – not Father John the Priest. He was always around and he played with us and had wonderful patience. John seemed to relish being the cool uncle." Each year he gave Patrick and his sisters an *experience* gift: whatever they wanted to do in the Bay area with John. He would take them to Great America; Marine World; a ferry ride to Angel Island. "It was always fun. John relished the fact that he was letting kids be kids."

"John for the forty plus years I've known him has been nothing but selfless; I think of all the things he did for us growing up; and for the community – the kids at PAL and those folks at San Quentin. His whole life has been about giving."

Although selfless, "John fights with himself over his machismo and his ego; he beats himself down if he feels like he is getting a little too big for his britches." Patrick says John is not perfect but instead "trying hard to do the right thing every day. He is not a Mother Theresa but someone who is real and trying to figure things out. The Bible provides wonderful examples of how to live like Christ but in my case I got more from watching John than from any written word."

Patrick and Pam organized John's post-stroke apartment clean-out and discovered a snapshot of what matters to John and what doesn't. "He had a probably thirty-year old mattress on the floor, hand-me-down couches and end tables that were probably ten, fifteen, twenty years old *before* he got them from his parents. They had some utility and that's all he needed; it was good enough for him. As a humble person, worldly trappings are not important. But what did matter was every single letter he got from someone, especially those from San Quentin and materials from Kairos which were all stacked up on the kitchen table."

Volunteers from Police Activities League, the soccer kids, Rotarians and many friends swarmed in to empty his old apartment after important belongings were removed. The old mattress, furniture not even suitable for charity, stacks of newspapers and miscellaneous debris filled a twenty-cubic-yard debris box – not surprising for a bachelor. New furnishings were contributed by his many friends and supporters for his new apartment.

Patrick brought John back to San Quentin eight weeks after his stroke and "he got a massive standing ovation in the prison church when the priest welcomed him back. It was very touching for him." An African-American man later said to Patrick, "One thing I absolutely love about John Kelly is that, from the first time that I met him, the color of my skin never mattered. From the first time I met him he was my brother."

Elaine Leeder co-leads with John Kelly a San Quentin program, New Leaf on Life. *She is Dean of Social Sciences and Professor of Sociology, Sonoma State University and author of* My Life with Lifers.

Elaine Leeder: "I was blown away by how the men in prison responded to him. He looks like a rock star around the San Quentin campus," a university except that everyone is locked up. She says everybody knows him – across the yard, "John, John, John," they all want to talk to him. She says he can't move more than a few feet and somebody else is approaching him to tell him about this and about that. She thought, "This is a remarkable man because he is so well liked." She started to work with him and began to see John's humanity, as a decent and generous soul. "He embraces people as they are, not for what they did. And he sees the good in every human being. And the guys respond to that; they really see that he respects and loves them in the full sense of his Christian background." Elaine is Jewish, but sees Catholic John and totally understands what it's like for somebody "who lives a truly spiritual Christian life."

Elaine calls John a man who cares about others, who is dedicated to helping others transform and who is a good human being. In Yiddish she says they have a term for that: mensch, a person of strength and honor. She says a mensch is "a person with soul, a person with depth, a person with substance, a person to whom you could turn and trust. That's what John is. He is truly a mensch."

He embraces everybody and in kind everybody embraces him. If there were more John Kellys in the world we would not be having the kinds of violence and troubles that we now have. "I wish we could clone him." But John says he gets more out of it than the guys do. So when he walks into that prison, the way he looks so close to those guys, it really is because they love him and he knows it, he feels it. I think that as a single man in the world "he created a far bigger family than any of us have in our blood family."

Elaine says that she is thrilled "that John is being honored by his story being told because he is a remarkable man. A biography is a way of cloning him; some way of noting what he has done. And some, hopefully, will pick up his example. There is good and evil in this world and John is good."

Elaine noted when she spoke to the San Mateo Rotary that everybody knew John and everybody wanted to honor him. "I mean here is this eccentric dude, you gotta say John is a dude, which is why I love him. I am drawn to people who are edgy, and he is edgy good." She says that he is not of the mainstream and that is to his credit. She loved to see John embraced as well in Rotary as he is in prison. "He finds the spark of humanity in each person and the rest of us should model that."

Sue Lempert: Former San Mateo Mayor says, "John typically doesn't talk much at Rotary Club but one day he talked about why he left the priesthood. He wasn't kicked out. He's not gay. Just moral reasons are why he did it. So if there is any real follower of Jesus, it is John. He really cares about the downtrodden; he really does. Not for political reasons or anything else. He is a wonderful human being."

Brian Cahill: He worked with John for years at San Quentin and says: "Yes, John can be crusty and cantankerous but most of us know it's really an act. While he would be the last person in the world to see himself as a saint, I believe he is, perhaps not in the tradition of canonized saints (he would turn it down if it came from the official church), but more along the lines of Dorothy Day (see en.wikipedia.org/wiki/Dorothy_Day). Like her, John lives his life with a passion for charity, justice and a full-bore commitment to the poor, marginalized and vulnerable among us."

Walter Heyman: "I once asked John why he left the priesthood and was told he left the Church – but not Christianity – 'because the Church today is trying to solve present-day problems with medieval methods.'"

Susan Manheimer: John has touched so many youth, but for her John is a "personification of all the Ten Commandments and of all our great social values. John will tell you, 'I'm no saint,' and, 'I'm not involved in this as a mission. I'm just merely doing what I was put here to do.'" She thinks John has this innate sense of helping those most in need.

Jerry Forbes: John is very focused. "He gets things done that you never think will happen. But all of a sudden he'll have people on his side and to this day you don't know how it happened. Samaritan House was an example. There were not many people particularly interested. It was a struggle to get people together to start doing the Samaritan House work. He knows how to get the right people."

Jerry describes John as "a sometimes cranky old man who has a heart of gold. He doesn't show it but does it in his actions." John says "don't praise me." But he's doing things he needs to be praised for. "What little money he has he often uses to help someone else. The man is a giver."

Senator Jerry Hill: "John Kelly has committed his life to helping those less fortunate. He has been a role model for the community, an exemplary citizen, and he has sensitized so many of us to the plight of our fellows. Our community is better because of John Kelly."

Bill Schwartz: "John is a natural leader. I would follow him anywhere he told me to go and not that many people have that effect on me. He is very persuasive. He is fully involved himself. And that is why he was so successful building the Samaritan House organization over the years. He worked well with people and in particular he had motivational skills. He was the head dog, the alpha male. We followed him and it was always a pleasure."

Peggy Myers: John is "an incredible man who has done incredible work, especially with children and schools." She thinks John's first love is working with kids in trouble and people in prison. He is so dedicated and still goes to San Quentin. "He does not like to talk about himself and all that he does but he is a wonderful man because he has touched so many people."

Jeanne Elliott: Forgiveness and humanity are the themes of John's work and these have been emblematic in all efforts of John Kelly. "He accepts us for who we are and helps us do good deeds without giving us a hard time about our failing."

Bill Kenney: "John is a well educated, bright gentleman. He is very charitable and very forgiving – certainly with all those San Quentin prisoners. He believes many of the prisoners can be rehabilitated."

Red Moroney: John and Kairos have been very successful at San Quentin in particular. In fact recidivism rates of people who have been through the Kairos program are "like thirty-six or thirty-seven percent as opposed to the general population which is about seventy-seven percent. The Kairos program is starting to get the attention of the administration and people in the corrections field."

Hope Whipple Williams: "John knows how important it is for teens to be successful adults and has mentored many children, youth and teens over his years. He is compassionate, caring, and like the Energizer Bunny, he keeps going and going in spite of his health issues. John is a legend in the greater San Mateo Community and we can never repay him for his services over the years."

Don Kelly: John's brother, takes great pride in John's "dedicated work and accomplishments for the underprivileged. He has a sincere heart and concern for the downtrodden, and he applies this concern in loving commitment every single day of his life."

John Kelly *(gets the final words):*
John says he gets nervous about this biography because he's trying "to keep his ego under control." He struggles with his emotions. He says the lifestyle of being a priest left out a lot of humanity and "when you try to put life back together after priesthood, it is really a challenge." And he worries that he is getting old and can't remember it all. But he does remember some "great adventures."

"If we are getting anything out of this biography process, it should be to develop a sense of the need to really get beyond a lot of the aspects of our culture like greed and selfishness and competition to the point where we realize our basic purpose is to help one another." John says, "The most important thing you can do is help another human being." John sees so many people who have ability, and he wants to see those abilities blossom. That's what drives him.

John says now that we have mass media and mass communications, our main responsibility is to "compare notes and to come to the common understanding of who we are." We should avoid saying to other cultures: "I got it right, you got it wrong; either believe it my way or you are never going to make it to heaven."

And for our local community responsibility, "you help the kids before they get in trouble. You help them think about who they are and what they want to become. The guys in San Quentin screwed up in their youth but some are at the point where they think about who they are and who they want to be. In many ways inmates are delayed adolescents. Practically speaking the earlier you can get people rethinking the better."

John claims that he has the same feeling now when he walks into San Quentin prison as when he taught at Serra High School. Many inmates stop and say hello and give John a slap on the back. He feels that he gets a lot of unconditional love in that building. He says if they try to thank him he says, "Forget it. I'm getting a payoff here, buddy. I don't need your thanks."

Appendix A

Letters from San Quentin

January 24, 2008

To my young people,

I write to you from a place that is full of murderers, thieves, rapists, snitches, wife beaters, and the dangerous prisoners in all of California, if not in the nation. This is but one of many such places.

When I was around some of your ages I never would have imagined spending the rest of my life in here. I came to prison at 19 years old. I got arrested at 17, but that isn't the worst of it. I had no prior arrests and was sentenced as an adult. My name is Ke. I'm serving a 25 years to Life plus 2 years for a gang-related murder. I killed another teen from a rival gang. I'll be 32 this year, so you do the math.

I'm no angel. I did my share of hustling, GIA, fighting, cutting classes, smoking, and partying. At one time, I had colleges watching me for my athletic talent in football and baseball. That all went to hell when I decided kicking it with my homies was more fun and cool. Most of my life I grew up in low-income housing (the Projects, the Hood, whatever you want to call it). My pops left me and mom's when I was 6 and moms was never around. So I started kicking it with the "Big Homies". For many years I held a lot of anger inside me because I felt everyone dissed me and I was nothing. The "Big Homies" showed me love, or so I thought.

When I committed this vicious murder, I felt hella scared because I stabbed this young kid to death. I ran to my homies house, but they were like, "you can't stay here." When I got jumped in at 16, I thought we would always have each other's backs forever! When I went to trial, my "boys" testified on me. I was more hurt than angry.

My story is like many up in here. My point or testimony for you young brothers is be careful who you kick it with and trust. Although pops and moms were never there for me out there when I needed them, they got my back now. The homies, now, are nowhere to be found.

You don't have to end up in my shoes. "Gangsta of the Year" or "I'm down" will only end in misery, pain, loneliness, a broken heart, and many tears. As I got older, I realized I was blind to the fact I was headed in the path of destruction. I destroyed many lives, including my own. Society nowadays has no mercy on the young people that act a fool or break the law(s). Communities are afraid and passing laws to lock you up for the rest of your life if you break any laws. I know this for a fact.

My prayer for you guys is to think about who you will hurt if you get locked up for life or get killed. At one time, I thoughts no one gave a damn about me, but I was wrong. Even if no one cares about you, you've got to care about yourself. Sometimes the worst enemy you could or ever will face is yourself. It is unfortunate it took me all these years and a life sentence to wake up. You don't have to end up like me or any one of these countless souls behind these guarded walls to make the right choices to live for yourself or your younger siblings or homies.

I promise you there is no glory for the soul that ends up here. What I can promise you is, if you get your education, a trade, or some positive skills your chances of prison life or an early death is minimum compared to those rolling the lock or just kicking it.

One last note. You know it isn't easy to ask for help if your boys, especially females, are around, but if you allow them to prevent you from getting your education, then you need to think about new homies and people that will help you instead of bring you down. Yeah, some of your boys will diss you, talk bad about you, and might even do things to bring you back (if you let them). You've got to dig/search within yourself for the strength to keep your dreams alive. It is my determination to keep God first in my life because He keeps me focused and strong.

I pray you will find some hope in this letter. Even though I'm serving a life sentence, my life is still alive and strong. I live on for you guys and in memory of my victims – my late brother, my family, my victim and his family, and others.

God Bless,
(signature)
"Ke"

To whom it may concern.   1/18/2008

This letter is to anyone who thinks there is something cool about gangs. I'm writing to tell you that gangs are not the answer to your problems. My name is Jerry Elster and I'm an ex-gang member from the Los Angeles area. I grew up in a large family and I felt that I wasn't getting my share of attention; it was as if I got lost in the crowd. It was pretty much the same way in school and around the neighborhood. I didn't feel as though I belonged anywhere. The gang seemed to be the answer to all my problems. They appeared to have accepted me for whom I was and never demanded too much of me. I've since learned that perceptions can be deceptive.

When people go to college they have expectations of achieving the knowledge and certification that will benefit them through out the rest of their lives. Patriots go off to fight for their country with the assurance that their contributions won't be forgotten. Their integrity and moral standards are pretty much respected and recognized by everyone. People enter the corporate world with high standards and usually a nice salary, not to mention the side benefits of paid vacations and medical coverage, for both them and their family. They happily all sign on the dotted line. Gang members don't usually require a signed contract right?

I'm in prison for taken' the life of a rival gang member. I have been incarcerated for twenty four years, two months, and eleven days. Not one of my homiez has ever so much as sent me a post card. Their expectations and demands far exceed the occupations and educational opportunities mentioned above. The gang demands not only your life but the lives of your family and friends. When your love ones are in your company, or even recognized as being related to you, their lives are in danger. The only ones who have been of any support to me are my family members.

As a life term inmate I'm just marking time, while the world passes me by, and all my family members die off. When you join a gang you jeopardize the lives of your loved ones and then they are the very ones you depend on to pick up the pieces when you take a fall (go to jail) or die. I know they didn't sign up for this. Gangs demand so much from you and give very little in return; they don't even offer the side benefits of paid vacations or medical insurance. I can't speak for you but I think I made a big mistake with this gang thang. What do you think?

With Respect

Big 'G'

Tom Huening

End of the Road
by Felix Lucero
1/5/2008

I dropped out of school at the age of fifteen. My excuse
then was that I had to take care of my new born daughter. It
wasn't a lie, but it was only half the truth. I was simply at
the end of a road that began in the seventh grade.

I made to significant discoveries at twelve: Girls and Gang
banging. It was for me to make the switch from honor student
to "at risk youth" to steal a term used by teachers and
counselors to describe a child who will either end up dead or
warehoused in on of California's many human waste camps because
most of my friends were coming along for the ride.

Every adult in my life became the enemy, especially my mom.
After school she would always scream, "did you do your homework
yet?" Of course the truth was that in the three hours between
getting out of school and her coming home from work the only
thing I did was smoke a joint and mess around with my girlfriend.

Instead of going to school I went to parties with the home boys.
Instead of carrying school books I carried a sawed-off shotgun.
The first time I realized that I wanted more than mediocrity
out of life was at my friend Joe's funeral. Joe was sixteen.
His girlfriend was standing next to his casket holding his son.
Little Joe was wearing a shirt that read "God Bless my Daddy."

I had potential, at least that what my teachers like to say.
But it wasn't enough to just want a better life, I had to make
the changes necessary to achieve my goal. One of the greatest
mistakes you can make in life is to do what is called walking
on the fence. I worked and night and went to school during the
day. However, there still existed in me this philosophy that
I had the right to sell drugs and carry a gun because my
environment and circumstance left me no other choice.
I went out drinking at a friends house one night. He was one
of those guys who's parents let him drink and guns in the house.
Before I left home my mom gave me speech about preparing for
the future and staying off the streets. A few hours later I
was sitting in a police station listening to a detective tell
me that I was under arrest for murder. I only took half a second
to destroy two lives.

Thirteen years later, at the age of twenty-nine, I'm STILL
paying for the sins of my youth. In six months I'll earn a
Liberal Arts degree graduating with nearly straight A's. I've
learned that education is important because it not only creates
opportunities for success in life, but it opens your eyes to
a bigger and more interesting world. I've had two essays published
and there's an exhibit in the San Francisco Public Library
currently displaying my work along with several other prisoners.
But my success is overshadowed by a fifteen-to-life sentence.
I don't know when or if I will ever get out of prison.

I tell my story to young men in a youth diversion program that
is held on Saturdays inside of San Quentin prison. I remind
then of their potential and their story. Everyone has a story.
I also show them the almost certain future of high school drop
outs. Some of them feel the message, and some of them become
me.

Tom Huening

01-17-08

COMO ESTAS MUCHACHOS,

GETTING STRAIGHT TO THE POINT. MY NAME IS TWIN & I AM 31 YEARS OLD & DOING 10 YEARS FOR CARJACKING & ASSAULT WITH A DEADLY WEAPON. I STARTED COMING TO JAIL AT THE AGE OF 11 FOR THINGS THAT ME & MY FRIENDS THOUGHT WERE FUN. NATURALLY I KNEW RIGHT FROM WRONG BUT I THOUGHT THAT STEALING, SMOKIN WEED & DESTROYING OTHER PEOPLE'S PROPERTY WASN'T AS SERIOUS AS STABBING, KILLING OR RAPING SOMEBODY. I ALSO THOUGHT THAT I WOULDN'T GET CAUGHT.

BY THE TIME I WAS 14 I BECAME A FULL-FLEDG CRIMINAL: A GANG BANGER, JACKER & DRUG DEALER. MY HOMEBOYS (& WHAT THEY THOUGHT ABOUT ME) BECAME MY PRIORITY. I PUT MORE FOCUS ON THEM THAN I DID ON THE CONSEQUENCES OF MY ACTIONS & NOT TO MENTI MY "REAL FAMILY" WHOSE LOVE & CONCERN FOR ME BECAME CLOUDED BECAUSE OF MY IMMATURITY.

TO MAKE THIS LONG STORY SHORT. 20 YEARS OF MY LIFE HAS BEEN SPENT IN & OUT OF JAIL BECAUSE OF MY INABILITY TO BE MY OWN MAN

All of you guys are pretty much grown men. Start getting used to taking charge of your life now (i.e., part time job, save money, volunteer in the community, etc.). Whatever your dreams are pursue them w/ everything you got. Don't be discouraged by another's advantages or what others have prejudged you as. Life is a blessing. God has given you many gifts (use them wisely & w/ reverence). Prison isn't a place where you can enjoy life or maximize the potential of your gifts. If anybody tells you different, he is a liar.

On that note I'm out. Stay strong & focus.

Sincerely,
Twin

Tom Huening

I've been incarcerated 22 years. When I was your age, my dreams and goals were to become a professional athlete. It wasn't for the fame or fortune but for the notoriety. I wanted to give back to the people who were less fortunate than I was and I knew I would be able to achieve that goal if I stayed in school, listened to my parents and teachers and kept believing in myself.

We have choices in life. We can choose to play by the rules and succeed or go against them and fail. When I was a freshman in high school I was getting good grades in most of my classes. I also was excelling in sports. When I turned 14 years old my friends asked me if I wanted to smoke a joint. I immediately said, "No! Are you crazy?" Well, about a week or so had past and then he asked me again and again. I eventually said yeah, let's do it. That was the biggest mistake I've ever made in my life. I never thought I would end up in prison but that's exactly what happened when I chose not to play by the rules. Now I look back from a different perspective - a perspective tempered by time, distance and maturity. I regret my behavior and I am saddened by the realization that I gave up. I haven't used drugs in over 20 years now and things in my life are good today. You know, I might not be a professional athlete but my dreams and goals are coming true.

It is very important for you to continue your education. Whenever you have the opportunity get involved into playing sports even if you are not so good at it because it will give you the ability to see the things you need to know about yourself, about others and about life. Education and sports will build your confidence by celebrating your small successes and victories. As you grow, you will come to understand humility as acceptance of both your assets and your liabilities. Furthermore, it is a healthy environment for growth because you will be able to turn anxiety into peace, anger into joy, tension into love, fear into faith, and guilt into trust.

You kids are special so don't ever forget that you are okay just the way you are. Your family and friends believe in you and so do I. In closing, I would like to leave you with this thought, "Someone will always be looking at you as an example of how to behave. Don't let that person down". Take care.   Bert

From the desk of
Paul Jordan

Greetings from San Quentin! I was asked to write a letter to a group of youngsters, something I've never done, so hang in there while I share my thoughts. Before I say anything let me first let you know that this letter is not meant to be a sermon. My intentions are to share a few thoughts and opinions about the world as I see it and hopefully in the process get you all to think. As stated above, my name is Paul. I have been locked up since 1994 for murder. I don't know when I'm getting out. I have two children, a daughter that is 19, and my son is 14. I came into prison with an attitude about the world that was clouded in ignorance, thinking I knew everything, not wanting to hear it from anyone, but realized that all that outward arrogance was really a mask I was hiding behind.

I grew up the youngest of seven children with four older brothers who thought it was their duty to kick my ass every chance they got. By the age of six I learned that by punching someone hard in the face you get them to leave you alone. By third grade I had been in a dozen fights, by the end of 8th grade I was a big kid so that when I entered high school I was ready to take on anyone. My favorite targets were seniors, preferably if they were on the football team. I was not just a fighter; I was also an athlete. I played basketball since 5th grade and by junior high I had become very good, winning all tournament trophies, leading my team in scoring, and loving it. I was a big kid and I felt a sense of confidence that people probably mistook for arrogance. When I hit high school I was ready for anything and had big plans. I was going to play ball and then play college ball. I started varsity as a sophomore and was the second leading scorer on my team. At this time I began smoking pot, drinking, partying, hanging out with the girls, and something else happened: I stopped getting better. My grades went all bad, and all around things started getting bad for me. I no longer thought about college. In fact, I had convinced myself that I wasn't college material. At this point my parents split up and I bounced back and forth, playing them against each other, fighting and drinking and smoking pot every chance I got. The day I turned 18 I was on my own, totally unprepared to meet the challenges of taking care of myself.

Something happened to me when I had to begin to fend for myself; I grew up. I slowed way down on the partying, I hardly smoked pot, and I worked, quit fighting, and started believing that life would eventually be okay. But somewhere inside me I still had an attitude. If people disrespected me I would want to smash them and on occasion I did, For the most part, however, I was cool. I played city league hoops, worked, settled down, had a kid, built a house; life was good. Then one day I had an incident and ended up beating some guy in the head with a stick and killed him. In one moment of reacting poorly to a situation my whole life went from great to as bad as it gets. Dude was dead, I got a life sentence, and my kid lost his father, just like that in a split second. All this because I had this attitude about how you "deal with people." I realize now this attitude was the result of a lifetime of conditioning: growing up with brothers who were bullies; living in an area where violence was acceptable; watching T.V. and movies that depict violence as macho; and a million other little influences that corrupted my thinking. Everyone loses when someone gets hurt, and people get hurt when you solve problems with violence.

I've learned many lessons in prison over the past 13+ years. The main one is that you are what you think you are. I used to tell myself I wasn't college material and I believed that. It took me coming to prison and being in a situation where I was "allowed" to take college classes to learn I am a damn good student. People tell us all kinds of stuff about ourselves trying to define us. Things like "you're stupid," and "you're from the ghetto so keep an eye on him." This list is endless. The way I see it, I define who I am, not the cops, not the teacher, not my parents, me! And who I am is someone who regrets being corrupted into thinking I wasn't good enough because I now know I am plenty good to accomplish just about anything, just so long as I'm willing to work for it. Nothing in life comes easy. You don't win the lottery; that doesn't happen. You work and plan. If you live your life blaming others you'll be miserable. Sometimes things are just what they are. You can blame your parents, hate the cops, whatever, but in the end you have to face each day and figure out how to get through life. You can't do it through clouded lenses, meaning pot and alcohol or whatever ain't the answer. One of the main rules of nature is "survival of the fittest." That used to mean the strongest but now it means who will work and plan. There's absolutely nothing you guys can't do if you're willing to put forth the effort, ask for help, and put away the kid games. Good luck to you all!

I wanted respect! I wanted love, loyalty and a family!

So I hung out with people who could give me all of this, and I got it!

It was pretty cheap too! It only cost me a couple of trips to "juvy" and a few months away from my freedom. That was a small price to pay for all I was getting. Well, at least it seemed that way when I was 14 years old. I gave up two months of my freedom for 2 years of respect, love, loyalty and a family. Then, at 15 years old, I made the ultimate sacrifice for my new family, "MURDER"!

I'm 25 years old now and have spent the last 10 years of my childhood in prison. The good thing is that I still have my family - the respect, the love, and especially the loyalty. Yep, the family that told me to go to school, clean the house, do my homework and be good. Yeah, they're still here.

That other family that I made all those sacrifices for------- well, 4 of them snitched on me right after the murder, and none of them have even written me a letter since that day I left.

It c ost me a "15 YEARS TO LIFE" sentence in prison to realize who my real family was.

You don't have to make those same sacrifices!

During the last 10 years I've changed! I grew up! The judge, the DA, even society said i was a cold blooded murderer and deserved to die in prison. They were wrong! I was just confused and lost. But I'm not anymore. I've found myself ! I'm a good person who is smart, and caring, and loving, and loyal, and a person who wants to help people just like me. Because I understand! If I can change, so can you.

I'm now in college finishing my AA degree. I completed my G. E. D. I'm the vice-chairman of a group called S.Q.U.I.R.E.S. where we talk to troubled youth. I'm the chairman of the Marketing Committee for a group called the T.R.U.S.T. where we hold workshops to educate other men in prison.

I have taken so many other self-help groups that it would take me a full day to write down every one and explain them. I'm a certified tutor. I help other inmates get their G.E.D. I've done a lot of good things with my life. I

163

even got married! I've been married over a year now and my wife is a wonderful woman.

But I'm still in prison paying for my actions as a kid. The truth is I'll probably spend the next 10 to 20 years in prison paying for what I did when I was 15 years old.

One way or the other, you're going to change! But you don't have to spend the rest of your life paying for it !

David Monroe, Jr.

Appendix B
Photos

John and his brother Ray.

John with his father and siblings.

John's ordination ceremony.

Early priesthood.

In India.

At San Quentin.

Albert Odom II, III & young Alexandar

San Quentin yard.

John at Wedding of Sam and Debbie Vaughn

James Alexander.

CPSIA information can be obtained at www.ICGtesting.com
Printed in the USA
BVOW07s1036120913

331016BV00002B/7/P